Ebury press, an imprint of Ebury Publishing,
20 Vauxhall Bridge Road,
London SW1V 2SA

Ebury Press is part of the Penguin Random House group of companies
whose addresses can be found at global.penguinrandomhouse.com

Penguin
Random House
UK

Recipes by Vicki Smallwood on pages: 17, 18, 20, 21, 24, 44, 46, 50, 53, 54, 57, 64, 65, 66,
70, 74, 78, 82, 88, 92, 98, 100, 104, 106, 110, 112, 113, 114, 126, 130, 136, 144, 148
Photography by Howard Shooter on pages: 3, 4, 5, 7, 11, 14, 15, 19, 25, 31, 35, 41, 47, 51, 55, 59,
67, 71, 75, 85, 87, 88, 93, 97, 101, 105, 107, 111, 119, 123, 127, 131, 135, 139, 145, 149, 153
Photography by Antoni Ferguson on pages: 39, 59, 79, 83, 87, 89, 95, 97, 109, 115
Food styling: Vicki Smallwood & Sarah Hancocks
Design: Jim Smith Design Ltd
Editor: Lydia Good

First published by Ebury Press in 2017

www.eburypublishing.co.uk

A CIP catalogue record for this book is available from the British Library

ISBN 9781785037085

Printed and bound in Latvia by Livonia Print

THE

KILNER®

EST 1842

COOKBOOK

EBURY
PRESS

CONTENTS

INTRODUCTION

The Kilner® jar company was established in 1842 when an enterprising businessman, John Kilner, and his family created a company producing and selling bottles and containers for food and drink.

John Kilner, after many unsuccessful attempts, perfected the jar and lid system to create a vacuum that would thoroughly preserve fruit and vegetables. Little did he know back then that this unique patent would become the worldwide standard for food preserving, enabling fruit and vegetables to be available out of season and, most importantly, during the winter months.

Today, this simple but effective invention still shapes how we design and develop our jars. Food, and how it is stored, is still the starting point for all creative idea development and with 175 years experience we believe that our knowledge should be shared!

At Kilner®, innovation is always on our minds as we seek to make our iconic designs relevant for every generation, bringing form and function together seamlessly. So, we've curated this collection of some of our favourite recipes to give you even more ideas for your favourite jars. From essential equipment, to helpful hints and tips including how to safely sterilise your Kilner® Jars and bottles, processing and sealing and making your first preserve. Whether you're a novice or an expert, we hope to inspire you on your journey to tasty homemade produce.

We'd love to hear from you! Get in touch via our website or on social media and sign up to be one of our Kilner® Club members.

www.kilnerjar.co.uk
Instagram @kilner_uk

Useful Equipment to get you Started

Kilner Preserving Pan
Kilner Jam Tongs
Kilner Muslin Squares
Kilner Waxed Paper Discs
Kilner Clip Top Jars and Bottles
Kilner Screw Top Jars and Bottles,
plus extra seals
Kilner Jam Thermometer
Kilner Spiralizer
Kilner Butter Churner
Slotted spoon
Non-metallic spatula
Hand blender
Food processor

STERILISING YOUR KILNER JARS

Essential in the preserving process, sterilising jars and bottles is required to remove all traces of bacteria, yeast, fungi and other organisms. This means that when you use the jar for preserving, the food will remain fresh within the vacuum.

There are two methods you can use for sterilising Kilner® Clip Top Jars and Bottles, Kilner® Preserve Jars, lids and seals and it is up to you which method you choose but we recommend the water bath method as the most suitable.

The first step of sterilisation, regardless of which method you choose, is to check the jars or bottles thoroughly for damage such as cracks, breaks and chips. If you find any are damaged, you must discard them responsibly. Now follow one of the two sterilisation methods detailed. It is important that you only sterilise your jars, bottles and lids or seals for a short time before you are ready to fill them, to ensure that they remain warm for the filling process.

Method 1: Water Bath

Remove the lids or rubber seals from your jars and put to one side. Next, place the jars into a Kilner® Preserving Pan and fill the pan with cold water until the jars are covered. Bring to the boil and keep at the maximum temperature for ten minutes, turn off the heat and cover the pan to keep the jars warm until you are ready to fill them.

Place vacuum seal lids or rubber seals in a small pan and fill with 10cm of water, heat and simmer at 82°C for 10 minutes, turn off the heat and cover the pan until you are ready to seal the jars (page 9).

A note on the recipes

All serving sizes are approximations, and your final yield may vary batch to batch, year to year, according to produce size and taste. It might be handy to have an extra jar or bottle to hand in case the quantity makes more than expected.

SEALING AND PROCESSING

Method 2: Dishwasher

Remove the lids or rubber seals from your jars and place everything in the top rack of your dishwasher and run it on a hot wash. No detergent or cleaning solutions should be used.

Time your dishwasher cycle to finish just as you are ready to fill the jars, or leave the jars and lids or seals inside the dishwasher to keep warm until you are ready to fill them.

Important Notes

- Do not attempt to sterilise your Kilner® bottles and jars by pouring boiling water into them.
- Always take care when sterilising jam jars and handling hot jars and lids. Please use the appropriate equipment such as Kilner® Jam Jar Tongs.
- Kilner® does not advise sterilising your jars using the oven method, as ovens can harbour bacteria from food that is stuck on the oven. A conventional oven with a fan will circulate bacteria.
- Do not put hot jars directly onto cold surfaces as this could cause them to crack.

Sealing

Always seal your jars as soon as they are filled, unless otherwise specified in the recipes. Once each jar is filled, use a non-metallic spatula to remove any air bubbles by running it around the inside of the jar (between the food and the jar).

If you are using a Kilner® Preserve Jar, place the discs onto your jars, add the screw-top band and tighten. If you are using a Kilner® Clip Top Jar, place the rubber seals onto the top of the jar and close the clips.

Processing

Place the jar in a large Kilner® Preserving Pan and cover the whole jar with water, making sure that it is submerged by at least 2.5cm. Bring to the boil for 30 minutes. Once boiled, leave the water and jars to cool completely before removing. The process of boiling the jars in water adds extra heat to the contents, which allows a vacuum seal to form.

1

BUTTERS, DIPS, DRESSINGS, OILS, SAUCES & CONDIMENTS

Useful Equipment
Kilner Butter Churner
Kilner Butter Paddles
Kilner Muslin Squares
Kilner Preserving Pan
Kilner Funnel
Kilner Jars and Bottles
Kilner Waxed Paper Discs

HOW TO MAKE HOMEMADE BUTTER

Makes 150–175g
300ml double cream
Large handful of ice cubes

Surprisingly simple to produce, homemade butter is far tastier than shop-bought and can be flavoured with sweet or savoury ingredients.

1 Remove the cream from the fridge at least an hour, preferably 2 hours, before you begin making the butter, to allow it to come to room temperature.

2 Pour the cream into a Kilner® Butter Churner and secure the lid on top to create a seal. Using the handle, churn the cream for 5–12 minutes until it has formed into a thick pale yellow butter and has separated from the buttermilk.

3 Remove the lid and carefully pour the buttermilk into a separate jar or container – you can keep this in the fridge for up to a week for use in other recipes.

4 Transfer the butter to a bowl of iced water and use Kilner® Butter Paddles or your hands to massage it and gently squeeze out any excess buttermilk. Repeat this process twice, or until you have a firm lump of butter.

5 For deliciously flavoured butter, see the recipes on page 13.

6 Once you have flavoured your butter, mould it into shape using the butter paddles or your hands. Cover with greaseproof paper or place in a butter dish. Refrigerate for up to 2 weeks.

Chilli & Lime Butter

Top grilled salmon or tuna steaks with this zesty-spiced butter, or add to barbecued corn on the cob.

115g Homemade Butter (page 12)
½ tsp crushed chilli flakes
2 tsp grated lime zest, plus extra
  to taste
Squeeze of lime juice
Pinch of sea salt

Parmesan, Basil & Tomato Butter

This Mediterranean-style butter is perfect for stirring into fresh pasta, or spreading on top of garlicky chicken.

115g Homemade Butter (page 12)
2 tsp grated Parmesan cheese
8–10 fresh basil leaves, shredded
1 tbsp chopped sundried tomatoes
Pinch of sea salt

Cinnamon & Honey Butter

This tasty butter is delicious melted onto pancakes or waffles for the perfect weekend brunch.

115g Homemade Butter (page 12)
60g honey
¼ tsp ground cinnamon
Pinch of sea salt

1 Remove the butter from the fridge an hour before use to soften and bring to room temperature. Check that it is free from any excess buttermilk.
2 Place the butter in a bowl and add your chosen flavourings, along with the salt.
3 Using your Kilner® Butter Paddles or your hands, mix all the ingredients thoroughly together to combine. At this point you should check the flavour of the butter. If you wish to make the flavours stronger, add in a little more ingredients (such as chilli flakes or cinnamon). Mould into shape if you wish.
4 The butter is now ready to be served. Serve straight away or cover with greaseproof paper or place in a butter dish. Refrigerate for up to 1 week.

FLAVOURED
BUTTER
OUR FAVOURITE
COMBINATIONS

CASHEW NUT BUTTER

Makes 300g
300g cashew nuts
Scant tbsp olive oil
Pinch of sea salt

Easy to make and even easier to eat, this delicious nut butter is perfect if you are cutting back on dairy or even dairy intolerant. Look out for broken cashews – they are often much cheaper and equally suitable for this recipe.

1 Preheat the oven to 180°C/Gas 4. Meanwhile spread the nuts out over a large baking sheet and bake in the oven for approximately 10–12 minutes, turning halfway through, until evenly toasted.
2 Leave the nuts to cool fully, then tip into the bowl of a small food processor and blend until very finely chopped and starting to clump together (this will take several minutes). You will need to stop the machine and scrape the sides down at intervals with a spatula.
3 Add the oil as the machine is running and continue to blend until a smooth paste forms. Season to taste and then spoon into a sterilised Kilner® Clip Top Jar (page 8). Store in a cool place and use within a month.

HUMMUS WITH CAYENNE & LEMON

So easy to make and perfect as a healthy snack served in a bowl with vegetable sticks and strips of toasted pitta bread. Also great in sandwiches and wraps.

1 Place the chickpeas, garlic, lemon zest and juice, tahini, olive oil, paprika and ground cumin in the bowl of a food processor or blender. Pulse until smooth.

2 If the mixture is too thick, add a little water and continue to pulse until you have the desired consistency. Season with salt to taste. Spoon into a sterilised Kilner® Jar (page 8), sprinkle over the cayenne pepper and chill until ready to serve.

Makes 350g

400g can chickpeas in water, drained and rinsed
1 garlic clove, peeled and roughly chopped
Finely grated zest and juice of 1 lemon
3 tbsp tahini
2 tbsp olive oil
½ tsp paprika
½ tsp ground cumin
Sea salt to taste
¼ tsp cayenne pepper

BEETROOT & MINT DIP

Makes 325g

1 beetroot, cleaned and
    trimmed (approximately 250g
    in total)
100g canned cannellini beans,
    rinsed and drained
3 tbsp chopped fresh mint
2 tsp balsamic vinegar
Pinch of sugar
2 tbsp crème fraîche, optional
Sea salt and freshly ground black
    pepper

**This colourful dip is the perfect summer snack. Serve with
pitta strips or carrot sticks or just spread it in a sandwich before
topping with salad leaves for a light lunch.**

1 Preheat the oven to 180°C/Gas 4. Wrap the beetroot in foil and roast
in the centre of the oven for about 1¾ hours until tender. Leave until
cool enough to handle, then peel and roughly chop.
2 Place the chopped beetroot in the bowl of a blender or food processor
along with the beans, 2 tablespoons of mint, balsamic, sugar and crème
fraîche, if using. Pulse until finely chopped. Stir through the remaining
mint and season to taste.
3 Spoon the mixture into a sterilised Kilner® Jar (page 8) and refrigerate
until ready to serve (best served at room temperature). Use within 5 days.

TAMARIND DRESSING

Makes 200ml
25g soft dark brown sugar
4 tbsp boiling water
1 shallot, peeled and finely
    chopped
25g fresh root ginger, peeled
    and finely grated
1 garlic clove, peeled and
    crushed
5 tbsp sunflower oil
2 tbsp tamarind concentrate
1 tbsp nam pla (fish sauce)
1 tbsp rice wine vinegar

Tamarind is commonly used in Thai and Indian dishes, but it is popular all over the world. Its sweet/sour flavour works well in both savoury and sweet dishes. Drizzle over stir-fried vegetables, chicken or salmon.

1 Dissolve the sugar in the boiling water, then add to the remaining ingredients.
2 Mix well to combine and allow to cool before pouring into a sterilised Kilner® Jar (page 8). Keep refrigerated and shake well before use. Use within 1 week.

VIETNAMESE DRESSING

Makes 140ml
Juice of 1 lime
2 tbsp rice vinegar
1 tbsp nam pla (fish sauce)
1 tbsp soft dark brown sugar
2 tbsp water
1 red chilli, deseeded and finely
    sliced
1 garlic clove, peeled and finely
    chopped

This dressing is delicious served over thinly sliced steak or large prawns. Alternatively, toss through a coleslaw instead of mayo.

1 Mix together the lime juice, rice vinegar, fish sauce and soft brown sugar in a bowl until the sugar has dissolved. Add the water, chilli and garlic.
2 Pour into sterilised Kilner® Clip Top Bottles (page 8) and store in the fridge. Shake before serving and use within 7 days.

PEPPER & HERB OIL

Make sure the herbs are thoroughly dry (rinse and pat dry with kitchen paper) before making this or the oil will spoil. Delicious drizzled over pizza or stirred through pasta that needs something extra! Alternatively pour into a small bowl, add a little balsamic vinegar and use for dipping bread.

1 Place all the ingredients in a frying pan set over a gentle heat and cook until the oil is hot and the herbs are starting to sizzle.
2 Allow to cool before pouring into a sterilised Kilner® Jar (page 8), then leave to marinate for 1 hour. Seal and store in a cool dark place. Shake before using, and use within 1 week.

Makes 150ml
15g fresh basil (leaves only),
   roughly torn
15g fresh oregano (leaves only),
   roughly torn
1 tbsp black peppercorns,
   crushed
130ml olive oil
Sea salt to taste

SWEET CHILLI KETCHUP

Makes 750ml

1kg cooking apples, skin on, cored and roughly chopped (reserve the cores and pips)

2 Scotch bonnet peppers, deseeded and roughly chopped

4 bird's-eye chillies, deseeded and roughly chopped

5cm piece of fresh root ginger, peeled and roughly chopped

450ml cider vinegar

450ml water

500g–1kg preserving sugar

Juice of 2 limes

1 red pepper, deseeded and finely diced

2–3 tbsp liquid pectin, optional

This is such a popular condiment you will find yourself putting it on the table at most mealtimes if chillies are your thing.

1 Blitz the apples and chillies in a blender or food processor to a coarse mash. Put in a large heavy-based stainless steel pan with the apple cores and pips, ginger, vinegar and water.

2 Bring to the boil and simmer for 30 minutes. Tip into a Kilner® Muslin Square or fine metal sieve and leave to drip into a bowl overnight. Measure the liquid back into the pan, and for each 600ml, add 500g preserving sugar. Add the lime juice and gently heat, stirring until the sugar has dissolved.

3 Bring to the boil. After 10 minutes add the red pepper and boil for a further 5–10 minutes until you have a pouring consistency. If this is proving hard to reach (chillis can be difficult!), stir in the pectin and try again.

4 Leave the ketchup to cool for 2–3 minutes before transferring to sterilised Kilner® Bottles (page 8). Note: the peppers will rise to the top if you don't allow the ketchup to cool first. Store in a cool, dark place and use within 6 months.

TOMATO & BASIL SAUCE

Makes 2.5 litres

3.5kg ripe tomatoes
1 tsp olive oil
½ onion, peeled and chopped
2 garlic cloves, peeled and finely
   chopped
A handful of fresh basil, finely
   chopped
3 tbsp lemon juice
1 tsp sea salt

The perfect standby sauce for pasta, fish or chicken.

1 Rinse and pat dry the tomatoes on kitchen paper, then cut into quarters, removing the cores.
2 Heat the oil in a frying pan and fry the onion and garlic until transparent. Add the tomatoes, bring to the boil and simmer for 20 minutes, stirring.
3 Purée the tomato mixture in batches. Strain through a metal sieve to remove the seeds and peel.
4 In a pan, bring the tomato purée and basil to the boil. Simmer, stirring occasionally, for about 30 minutes or until the sauce reaches the desired consistency. Finally, stir in the lemon juice and season to taste.
5 Ladle the sauce into sterilised Kilner® Jars, leaving 6ml space at the top. Remove air bubbles, seal and process for 30 minutes (page 9).

HOT CHILLI SAUCE

Makes 600ml

4 red bird's-eye chillies, deseeded
1 dried chipotle chilli
4 ripe tomatoes, quartered
1 carrot, peeled and chopped
1 small onion, peeled and chopped
1 celery stick, chopped
2 tbsp agave syrup or honey
1 tbsp tomato purée
2 tbsp red wine vinegar
1 tsp tamarind paste
150ml organic apple juice
5 tbsp water
Sea salt and freshly ground
   black pepper

This versatile sauce adds a kick to all kinds of barbecue meats, or fresh fish, especially tuna. Remember, a little goes a long way!

1 Place all the ingredients except the seasoning in a Kilner® Preserving Pan or large stainless steel saucepan. Bring to the boil, then cover and simmer gently, stirring occasionally for 45 minutes until pulpy.
2 Purée in a blender or food processor, scraping down the sides as necessary, then rub through a large metal sieve into a bowl. Season.
3 Transfer the sauce to 2 warm sterilised Kilner® Jars with non-metallic or vinegar-proof lids (page 8). Top with waxed paper discs, seal and leave to cool completely. Refrigerate for up to 1 month.

HOLLANDAISE SAUCE

Serve this classic sauce warm over poached eggs on toast, fish, seafood or vegetables such as asparagus.

1 Melt the butter in a stainless steel saucepan and pour into a heatproof jug. The clear, clarified butter will sit on top of the milk solids. Now take a sterilised 1-litre Kilner® Preserve Jar (page 8) and add the egg yolks. Add a splash of lemon juice and a touch of melted butter.

2 Insert a hand-held blender into the jar and begin blending. As you blend, slowly pour the clarified butter into the jar in a steady stream (don't worry if some of the milk solids also escape into the jar). Your sauce will emulsify and thicken as you add the butter. Once you reach the desired consistency (smooth and not too runny), stop adding butter.

3 Check the sauce and season to taste, adding more fresh lemon juice if desired. Serve straight away or store in the fridge for up to 2 days.

4 To reheat, gently microwave for 15 seconds then whisk, and repeat until warm. Or gently heat and whisk in a pan over simmering water.

Makes 180ml
125g butter
3 large free-range egg yolks
Juice of ½ lemon
Sea salt and freshly ground black
     pepper

WHOLEGRAIN MUSTARD

Makes 150ml

2 tbsp yellow or white mustard seeds
2 tbsp brown mustard seeds
100ml white wine or cider vinegar, plus extra as necessary (see method)
½ tsp sea salt
1 tsp sugar

Made with whole mustard seeds, this tasty mustard will enhance the flavour of all your dishes and goes particularly well with red meat and chicken. It is also perfect stirred into sauces and marinades.

1 To a small (non-metallic) container, Kilner® Jar or glass tumbler, add the mustard seeds and cover with the vinegar.
2 To prevent the kitchen smelling of vinegar, cover the container with clingfilm. Leave to stand for 3 days – do not refrigerate.
3 Check periodically – the seeds will swell as they absorb the liquid. Add additional vinegar to prevent them drying out – it does not matter if you add too much.
4 After 3 days, drain off the excess liquid and reserve.
5 Using a hand-held blender, food processor or pestle and mortar, grind the seeds to a paste. Add the salt and sugar and continue to blend. Add a little extra reserved liquid to get the mustard to a good consistency.
6 Transfer to sterilised Kilner® Jars (page 8) and, if possible, leave to mature for a few days before use. The mustard should keep for several months in a cool, dark place and does not need refrigerating.

APPLE SAUCE

Perfect with pork, but also in pastries!

1 Core each apple and cut into 2cm pieces. Place in a Kilner® Preserving Pan and coat with the lemon juice.
2 Stir in the sugar and add the water. Make sure there is enough water to cover the base of the pan – add more, if necessary.
3 Bring to the boil, reduce the heat and simmer, stirring occasionally, until the apples have softened (about 20 minutes). Spoon some of the mixture into a metal sieve set over a large bowl and pass through. Work in batches until all the mixture has been sieved.
4 Put the sieved apples in a large heavy-based stainless steel saucepan and bring to the boil. Reduce to medium–low and simmer, until hot.
5 Using a Kilner® Funnel, ladle the sauce into sterilised Kilner® Jars (page 8), leaving 5mm of space at the top. Remove any air bubbles using a spatula, then wipe the rims and threads of the jars clean and seal tightly (page 9).
6 Process the jars for 20 minutes (page 9).

Makes 1 litre
2kg cooking apples
   (Bramley work well here)
50ml lemon juice
60g sugar
50ml water

CRANBERRY SAUCE

Perfect with roast turkey or soft French cheese.

1 First, squeeze the juice of 1 clementine into a Kilner® Preserving Pan. Add the cranberries, sugar and port.
2 Cook over a medium heat for 4–5 minutes until the cranberries soften and burst, stirring occasionally. Segment the other clementine and remove the pith. Add to the pan and cook, stirring, for 2 minutes.
3 Transfer to a sterilised Kilner® Jar (page 8) and store in the fridge. Alternatively, freeze in a plastic container for up to 2 months.

Makes 300ml
2 clementines
200g cranberries
100g light brown soft sugar
6 tbsp port

2

PICKLES, RELISHES & CHUTNEYS

Useful Equipment

Stainless steel or enamel pans – always use these. This ensures that the vinegar does not react with your pan and cause a metallic taste.

Kilner Clip Top Jars and Bottles
Preserve Jars and Twist Top Jars
Kilner Preserving Pan
Colander
Jug
Kilner Jam Jar Tongs

CHECKLIST FOR PICKLES

Preparation: Always use wooden utensils and a pan made from stainless steel or enamel for pickling. This ensures that the vinegar does not react with your pan, giving a metallic taste. Always ensure that you rinse and drain your prepared fruit and vegetables after you have salted them.

Packing: To prevent your pickled vegetables or fruit from bruising, do not pack them too tightly. Leave a space of at least 1.5cm at the top of your jars. This allows for the vinegar to be added. Always use vinegar-proof lids when sealing jars to prevent a metallic taste forming. The Kilner® Clip Top Jars are perfect for pickles for this reason.

Storage: It is important to let your pickles mature in flavour before you open them. For best results, store in a cool, dry, dark place for at least 4 weeks before opening. The longer you leave it, the more intense the flavour will be. Once opened, keep refrigerated and use within 4 weeks, unless specified otherwise in the recipes.

CHECKLIST FOR CHUTNEYS

Preparation: Always use a pan made from stainless steel, and wooden utensils. Other materials may react with the vinegar and change the flavour and colour of your chutney.

Being precise about the size of your chopped fruit and vegetables makes for an attractive-looking chutney.

Cooking: Chutneys should be allowed a long and slow cooking time in an uncovered pan to allow them to become rich and smooth. Make sure you stir continuously to prevent the mixture from burning on the bottom of the pan.

Top tip: To check the chutney is ready for potting, run a wooden spoon through the mixture across the bottom of the pan to form a channel. If the channel holds after two seconds without the chutney flooding back in, the right consistency has been reached.

Storage: Chutneys are best eaten after a long period of maturing. We recommend storing them in a cool, dry, dark place for at least 8 weeks before opening. Once open, keep refrigerated, unless specified otherwise in the recipes.

PICKLED RED CABBAGE

Makes 1 x 1 litre Kilner Jar
1 medium red cabbage
1 tbsp salt
450ml distilled pickling vinegar
½ tbsp granulated sugar
½ small onion, peeled and sliced

Colourful crunchy, spiced cabbage is always good to keep in the pantry and goes perfectly with cold meats and casseroles.

1 Trim and slice the cabbage into quarters, discarding the outer leaves. Cut away the hard central core and shred the remaining cabbage finely.
2 Layer the cabbage in a mixing bowl with the salt, then cover with a tea towel and leave to stand overnight.
3 In a Kilner® Preserving Pan gently heat the pickling vinegar and sugar, stirring occasionally, until the sugar has dissolved. Set aside to cool.
4 The next day thoroughly rinse the cabbage to remove all traces of salt and pat dry with kitchen towel. Pack into a 1-litre sterilised Kilner® Clip Top Jar (page 8), adding a slice or two of onion as you go. Pour in the reserved vinegar until the cabbage is covered, leaving 1.5cm space at the top. Wipe the rim and threads of your Kilner® Jar and seal (page 9).
5 Process your Kilner® Jar (page 9). Leave to mature for 4 weeks in a cool and dry place.

PROBIOTIC BEETROOT & RED CABBAGE SAUERKRAUT

While probiotic supplements can help maintain good bacteria in your digestive system, fermented vegetables, such as this delicious sauerkraut, also do the trick and are a much tastier way to go!

Makes 1 x 0.5 litre Kilner Jar

½ medium red cabbage head, finely diced (reserve a leaf for sealing)

1 medium beetroot, peeled and grated

5cm piece of fresh root ginger, peeled and grated

1 tsp sea salt

1 Place the cabbage, beetroot and ginger in a large bowl and sprinkle with salt. Use your hands to scrunch the salt into the other ingredients. Cover with a tea towel and leave to rest for a few hours, mixing occasionally with your hands, until the juices collect in the bottom of the bowl.

2 Transfer the mixture to sterilised Kilner® Jars (page 8) and press down really well. If the juices don't completely cover the mixture, add more salted water (1 teaspoon of salt to 250ml of water). Be sure to leave around 4cm space between the liquid and the top of the jar.

3 Cover with a cabbage leaf and pack down again. Put the lid on and leave it loosely fastened, or if using a Clip Top, avoid fully fastening the clip.

4 Leave the jars out on your worktop out of direct sunlight for 3–7 days to mature (the longer you leave the sauerkraut, the stronger the taste and so if you are making this for the first time we recommend 3 days).

5 Once the fermenting process is complete, seal tightly (page 9) and refrigerate until chilled. The sauerkraut is now ready to eat and will keep in the fridge for months – if it lasts that long!

PICKLED RED ONION & LIME

Makes 1 x 1 litre Kilner Jar

5 medium red onions, peeled
   and sliced
500ml boiling water
2 limes, thinly sliced
300ml distilled pickling vinegar
2 tbsp granulated sugar
1 tbsp salt
1 tbsp peppercorns
1 tbsp dried coriander

A delicious condiment for sandwiches, burgers and meats.

1 Place the sliced onions in your Kilner® Preserving Pan and add the boiling water, ensuring the onions are fully submerged.

2 After 1 minute, drain the onions, transferring the liquid to a large heavy-based saucepan, and add the onions to your 1-litre sterilised Kilner® Clip Top Jar (page 8) with the slices of lime.

3 To the reserved liquid add the distilled pickling vinegar, sugar, salt, peppercorns and coriander. Boil for 5 minutes, stirring occasionally, to ensure all of the salt and sugar has dissolved.

4 Leave the boiling solution to cool for 10 minutes (DO NOT pour boiling water directly into your jar!), then add to the sliced onion and lime mixture until the liquid level is nearly at the top.

5 Seal the jar (page 9) and allow to cool before refrigerating. Your delicious pickled red onion and lime will taste best if left to sit for 24 hours … Enjoy!

SWEET & SOUR COURGETTES WITH RED ONION

Makes 1 x 0.5 litre Kilner Jar
3 courgettes, trimmed
2 red onions, peeled
2 tbsp salt

For the brine
400ml distilled malt pickling
    vinegar
200g granulated sugar
¼ tsp turmeric
2 tsp yellow mustard seeds
1 tsp coriander seeds
    (dry-roasted in a frying
    pan over a medium heat
    for a few minutes)

Delicious with thick crusty breads and hard cheeses or cold meats. A great addition to a picnic or a simple lunch.

1 Using a mandolin slicer, slice the courgettes into 5mm thickness. Again, using the mandolin slicer, slice the onions into 2mm rings.
2 Place the onion in a large bowl along with the courgette. Sprinkle with the salt and mix with your hands to coat. Cover with clingfilm and place in the fridge for about 3 hours.
3 Meanwhile, make the brine. Place the vinegar, sugar, turmeric, mustard and coriander seeds in a Kilner® Preserving Pan and bring to the boil. Turn the heat down and simmer for about 5 minutes. Remove the pan from the heat and let the brine cool to room temperature.
4 Leave the salt on the courgettes and onions and drain well. Fill sterilised Kilner® Jars (page 8) with the courgettes and onions. Pour in the prepared brine, ensuring that you leave at least 1.5cm space at the top. Tap the jars to remove any trapped air.
5 Wipe the rims and threads of your Kilner® Jars and seal (page 9). Process your Kilner® Jars (page 9). Allow to mature for 4 weeks in a cool and dry place.

KIMCHI

Makes 1 x 1.5 litre Kilner Jar
900g red cabbage, thinly sliced
50g pickling salt
225g daikon radish, julienned
225g carrot, peeled and
  julienned
6 spring onions, sliced into
  2.5cm segments
3cm piece of fresh root ginger,
  sliced or finely chopped
4 garlic cloves, finely chopped
1 Asian pear (or apple), peeled,
  cored and chopped
1 small brown onion, peeled
240ml water
30g gochugaru or cayenne
  pepper, adjust quantity to taste
2 tbsp nam pla (fish sauce)

Traditional recipes use a fiery Korean chilli powder called gochugaru. Try this adapted Kimchi recipe guaranteed to set your taste buds alight, but mild enough for those who prefer a little less heat.

1 Place the cabbage slices in a large bowl along with the pickling salt. Massage the leaves with the salt until they begin to release water.

2 Cover the cabbage with water and leave for a minimum of 2 hours, occasionally mixing with your hands (the cabbage will have reduced in volume and feel limp to the touch). Leave for another hour if still firm.

3 Strain the cabbage and rinse under running water, repeat and then return to the bowl. Add the daikon radish, carrot, spring onions, ginger and garlic.

4 In a food processor or blender, combine the pear or apple, brown onion, water, gochugaru or cayenne and fish sauce until smooth and add to the cabbage. Mix the contents of the bowl thoroughly, making sure everything is coated with the sauce.

5 Pack the Kimchi tightly into sterilised Kilner® Jars (page 8), leaving 2.5–5cm of space at the top. Make sure the vegetables are pushed down and compact so they are fully submerged.

6 Wipe the rims and threads of your Kilner® Jars. Close the jars with a loose-fitting lid (to allow the gases to escape) and leave to ferment at room temperature for a minimum of 3 days. After that, taste the Kimchi and decide when to stop the fermenting process according to your preferred level of sourness. Everyone is different but you will be looking for a definite sour or tangy taste. Once you have reached the required sourness, seal the jars tightly (page 9) and store in the fridge.

PICKLED ONIONS

Makes 1 x 1 litre Kilner Jar

500g small pickling onions
25g salt
600ml distilled malt pickling
  vinegar
100g granulated sugar
10 peppercorns
2 tsp mustard seeds
1 tsp coriander seeds
2 bay leaves

Pickling onions, whether homegrown or bought, is immensely satisfying and far easier than you might think.

1 Place the onions in a Kilner® Preserving Pan and pour over a kettle of boiling water. Leave for 20 seconds, then transfer to a colander, return to the pan and pour over lots of very cold water. The skins should now peel away easily.

2 Once peeled, place the onions in the preserving pan and sprinkle with the salt. Cover with a tea towel and leave overnight or for up to 24 hours.

3 Meanwhile, pour the vinegar and sugar into another preserving pan with the peppercorns, mustard seeds, coriander seeds and bay leaves. Bring to the boil, then remove from the heat. Cover with a tea towel and set aside overnight to allow the spices to infuse.

4 The following day, rinse the onions well and pat dry with kitchen paper. Pack into sterilised Kilner® Jars (1-litre Kilner® Clip Top Jar or 1-litre Kilner® Preserve Jar and see page 8), then use a jug to pour over the prepared vinegar and spices, completely covering the onions. Ensure that you leave at least 1.5cm space at the top.

5 Wipe the rims and threads of your Kilner® Jars and seal (page 9). Process your Kilner® Jars (see page 9). Allow to mature for 6 weeks in a cool and dry place.

> **Top tip:** Always use the freshest produce that has been thoroughly cleaned.

PICKLED CUCUMBER

A great addition to burgers, sandwiches and salads.

1 Slice the cucumber and shallot very finely and layer in a sterilised Kilner® Clip Top Jar. Scatter with dill.

2 In a jug, combine the sugar, salt, vinegar and mustard seeds, then pour over the cucumber and dill mixture, ensuring that you leave at least 1.5cm space at the top.

3 Wipe the rim and thread of your Kilner® Jar(s) and seal (page 9). Process your Kilner® Jar(s) (page 9). Allow to mature for 4 weeks in a cool and dry place.

Makes 1 x 0.5 litre Kilner Jar
½ cucumber
1 shallot, peeled
1 sprig of dill, chopped
1 tbsp granulated sugar
Pinch of salt
150ml malt vinegar
1 tsp whole mustard seeds

SWEET CUCUMBER PICKLE

This sweet condiment is good with all manner of salads and in sandwiches, but particularly with hot-smoked trout or salmon.

1 Using the slicing blade of a food processor or a very sharp knife, very finely slice the cucumbers. Slice the onions very thinly too. Combine the cucumber, onion and dill, if using, in a large bowl.

2 Mix the sugar, salt and vinegar in another bowl and pour over the cucumber and onion. Leave overnight for the sweet and sour flavours to mix and mingle. If that isn't possible, leave for at least 3 hours before serving.

3 Pack into a large sterilised Kilner® Clip Top or Twist Top Jar (page 8). Store in the fridge and once open, use within 2 weeks.

Makes 1 x 1 litre Kilner Jar
1kg cucumbers
3 small onions, red or white, peeled
1 tbsp chopped dill, optional
250g granulated sugar
1 level tbsp salt
200ml cider vinegar

ONION RELISH

Makes 1 x 0.5 litre Kilner Jar

3 tbsp olive oil

1kg red onions, peeled and
finely sliced

150g soft brown sugar

1 tsp black mustard seeds

1 tsp onion seeds

100ml balsamic vinegar

150ml red wine vinegar

Onion relish is delicious with burgers or spread thickly on cheese on toast. It's a great store cupboard standby to pep up all sorts of simple dishes. If you like a bit of heat with your onions, try replacing the onion seeds with a teaspoon of dried chilli flakes.

1 Heat the olive oil in a large heavy-based pan. Add the onions and fry gently until softened.

2 Take a piece of greaseproof paper, screw it up into a ball, open out and then run briefly under the cold water tap. Shake off any excess water and then cover the onions with it, tucking it around them in the pan, being careful not to burn yourself. Cook on a gentle heat for a further 30–35 minutes until the onions are thickened and reduced.

3 Discard the greaseproof paper and add the remaining ingredients to the pan. Bring to the boil and cook for about 40 minutes until the mixture has thickened and no pools of liquid remain.

4 Spoon the relish into a sterilised Kilner® Jar and seal (pages 8 and 9). Leave in a cool dark place to mature for at least 2 weeks before using and refrigerate after opening.

PICCALILLI

This salty-sour pickle goes perfectly with raised pies, cured meats or strong cheeses.

1 Place all the vegetables in a large non-metallic bowl. In a jug dissolve the salt in the water to make a brine and pour over the vegetables. Put a heavy plate on top of the vegetables to keep them submerged in the brine and leave for 24 hours.

2 The next day, drain the vegetables through a colander and rinse in cold water. Bring a large pan of water to the boil, add the vegetables and blanch for about 2 minutes – do not overcook as they should be crunchy. Drain and refresh in cold water to halt the cooking process.

3 To make the sauce, put the flour, sugar, turmeric and mustard powder in a small bowl and mix in a little of the vinegar to make a paste. Transfer to a Kilner® Preserving Pan along with the remaining vinegar and bring to the boil, stirring continuously so no lumps appear. Reduce the heat and simmer for about 15 minutes.

4 Add the vegetables to the prepared sauce and stir well so they are all coated. Ladle into warm sterilised Kilner® Jars (page 8), making sure there are no air gaps, seal (page 9) and allow to cool completely before labelling.

5 Store in a cool dark place. Allow the flavours to mature for 4 weeks and refrigerate after opening. Once open, the piccalilli will keep for up to 6 months.

Makes 2 x 1 litre Kilner Jars

1 large cauliflower, cut into florets

2 large onions, peeled, quartered and finely sliced firmly, or use pickling onions

900g mixed vegetables such as courgettes, runner beans, carrots and green beans, cut into bite-sized pieces

60g sea salt

1.2 litres water

2 tbsp plain flour

225g granulated sugar (increase this quantity slightly if you don't like the pickle too sharp)

1 tbsp turmeric

60g English mustard powder

900ml ready-spiced distilled pickling vinegar

SPICED APPLE & PEAR RELISH

Makes 2 x 0.5 litre Kilner Jars

900g cooking apples
(preferably Bramley), peeled,
cored and diced

600g pears, peeled, cored
and diced

500g light muscovado sugar

2 onions, peeled and finely
chopped

1 cinnamon stick

2 tsp ground ginger

1 tsp sea salt

700ml cider vinegar

This relish goes well with cold meats or cheeses, the perfect way to use up leftovers for a delicious sandwich!

1 Place all the ingredients in a Kilner® Preserving Pan set over a medium heat, stirring until the sugar has dissolved, then bring to the boil.

2 Continue cooking, stirring from time to time, until the mixture has thickened. When you can draw a wooden spoon through the mixture, leaving a trail that remains clear for a few seconds before any liquid appears, it is ready. Discard the cinnamon stick and divide between sterilised Kilner® Jars (page 8). Store in a cool dark place and use within 6 months.

APPLE & CRANBERRY CHUTNEY

Makes 1 x 1.5 litre Kilner Jar

1kg cooking apples (Bramley are good), peeled and cut into small chunks

500g eating apples, peeled and cut into large chunks

450g onions, peeled and sliced

50g fresh root ginger, peeled and finely chopped

1 tsp peppercorns

500g granulated sugar

250ml cider vinegar

500g cranberries

Goes perfectly with cheeses and cold meats at Christmas time.

1 Place all the ingredients apart from the cranberries in a Kilner® Preserving Pan and cook over a low heat, mixing well to dissolve the sugar.

2 Bring the mixture to the boil, then lower the heat and simmer without a lid for 50 minutes to 1 hour – be sure to stir well so that the chutney thickens.

3 Add the cranberries and simmer for 10 minutes but ensure that the cranberries do not split. Transfer the chutney straight from the pan into sterilised Kilner® Jars and seal (pages 8 and 9).

4 Store in a cool, dark place and use within 6 months.

MARROW CHUTNEY

Perfect when you have a glut of in-season marrows, this chutney goes well with all kinds of cheese and cold meats.

1 Peel and cube the marrow. Sprinkle generously with salt, cover with a tea towel and place in the fridge overnight.

2 Rinse very well the next day and place in a Kilner® Preserving Pan. Add the remaining ingredients and slowly bring to the boil.

3 Lower the heat and simmer, stirring occasionally, for 1–2 hours or until you see the consistency has thickened.

4 When you have the desired consistency, transfer the chutney into sterilised Kilner® Jars (page 8) and seal (page 9).

Makes 2 x 0.5 litre Kilner Jars

1.6kg marrow
Sea salt
300g sultanas
4 shallots, peeled and chopped
1 tbsp grated fresh root ginger
2 garlic cloves, peeled and
  crushed
400g light brown soft sugar
2 large cooking apples (Bramley
  are good), cored, peeled and
  chopped
375ml organic cider vinegar
1 ½ tbsp Dijon mustard
1 tsp chopped and deseeded
  chillies
1 tsp paprika

PINEAPPLE CHUTNEY

Makes 1 x 1 litre Kilner Jar

2 tbsp chilli oil

3 red onions, peeled and
    thinly sliced

1 tbsp black onion seeds

2 tsp fennel seeds

2 tsp turmeric

2 pineapples, peeled, cored
    and cut into small chunks

1 chipotle chilli, whole

3cm piece of fresh root ginger,
    peeled and finely chopped

250g granulated sugar

175ml malt vinegar

1 tsp sea salt

**This is best made when pineapples are cheap and plentiful.
If you want to reduce the heat a little, use sunflower oil in place
of the chilli oil.**

1 Heat the oil in a Kilner® Preserving Pan and gently fry the onions
and spices for 5 minutes until the onions have softened.

2 Add the remaining ingredients and simmer, stirring occasionally, for
about an hour until thickened and most of the liquid has evaporated.
When you draw a wooden spoon through the mixture you should be
able to see the base of the pan for a few seconds before the chutney
covers it once more.

3 Remove and discard the chilli before spooning the hot chutney
into sterilised Kilner® Jars and seal (pages 8 and 9). Leave to cool
completely before labelling. Store in a cool dark place. Once opened,
keep in the fridge.

HEARTY ONION
& ALE CHUTNEY

**Makes 4 x 0.25 litre
Kilner Jars**

400g onions, peeled and finely
sliced

250g swede, peeled and cut into
5mm pieces

250g cooking apples (Bramley
are good), peeled, cored and
chopped into 1cm pieces

150g cauliflower, cut into tiny
florets

2 fat garlic cloves, peeled and
crushed

100g pitted dates, finely chopped

150g tomato purée

300g demerara sugar

50g dark brown soft sugar

250ml malt or cider vinegar

2 heaped tbsp English mustard
powder

½ tsp ground mace (add to taste)

1 heaped tsp sea salt

½ tsp freshly ground black
pepper

500ml water

500ml traditional ale, bitter
or stout (not lager)

**A delicious accompaniment to any cheese board. Locally
brewed organic ale works particularly well in this recipe.**

1 Place all the ingredients except for the ale in a Kilner® Preserving Pan.
Simmer on a low heat, stirring constantly, until the sugar has completely
dissolved. Continue to cook for 1 hour to let the liquid reduce.

2 Remove the pan from the heat and pour 250ml of the ale, bitter
or stout into the pan, then return to a low heat for 30 minutes.
Pour in the remaining alcohol and cook for another 30 minutes.

3 Transfer the chutney to sterilised Kilner® Jars (page 8), ensuring
there are no air pockets in the mixture, then seal with vinegar-proof
lids (page 9). Store for 4–6 weeks in a cool dark place before opening.
Once open, keep in the fridge.

SWEET TOMATO CHUTNEY

A sweet/sour chutney which is easy to make at any time of year, as you can use fresh or canned tomatoes. However, the more watery the tomatoes, the less chutney you'll get. So, use fresh in summer and early autumn and save the canned ones for winter.

Makes 1 x 1 litre Kilner Jar

1 bulb of garlic, peeled and
   coarsely chopped
5cm piece of fresh root ginger,
   peeled and coarsely chopped
120ml balsamic vinegar
2 x 400g cans tomatoes or
   900g fresh tomatoes, skinned
   and coarsely chopped
240ml red wine vinegar
350g granulated sugar
1 tsp salt
1 tbsp tomato purée
1 tsp cayenne pepper (add to taste)
100g sultanas

1 In a food processor or blender, pulse the garlic, ginger and balsamic vinegar until smooth, then set to one side.

2 Add the tomatoes, red wine vinegar, sugar and salt to a Kilner® Preserving Pan. Bring slowly to the boil, then reduce the heat to a gentle simmer and add the tomato purée and the garlic and ginger mixture, stirring well to combine.

3 Simmer for about 2 hours to allow the liquid to reduce and the mixture to thicken, stirring from time to time. As the mixture thickens, stir more frequently to prevent burning on the base of the pan.

4 Once thickened (page 33), add cayenne pepper and the sultanas.

5 Spoon into sterilised Kilner® Jars and seal (pages 8 and 9). Leave to cool completely before labelling. Store in a cool dark place for up to 6 months. Once opened, store in the fridge and use within 1 month.

Skinning fresh tomatoes: Using a sharp knife, score a small cross in the bottom of the tomatoes. Prepare one bowl of boiling water and one bowl of ice water. Working in batches, carefully submerge the tomatoes in the boiling water using a slotted spoon and leave for 45–60 seconds, until the skin starts to wrinkle. Scoop them out with the slotted spoon and plunge them into the ice water so that they are cool enough to handle, lift them directly back out and simply peel off the skin.

BANANA CHUTNEY

**Makes 3 x 0.5 litre
Kilner Jars**

4 tbsp vegetable oil

2 onions, peeled and chopped

2 red bird's-eye chillies, deseeded
and finely chopped

4 garlic cloves, peeled and finely
chopped

2 tsp ground turmeric

1 tsp curry powder

8 bananas, peeled and sliced

150ml cider vinegar

30g muscovado sugar

1 tbsp pomegranate molasses

1 tbsp dark soy sauce

**This is a perfect accompaniment to any sort of curry but also
works just as well with cold meats.**

1 In a Kilner® Preserving Pan heat the oil over a medium heat and fry
the onions until softened. Add the chillies, garlic and spices to the pan
and stir to coat. Cook gently for 5 minutes until softened and fragrant.

2 Add the sliced bananas, vinegar, sugar, pomegranate molasses and soy
sauce and bring to the boil. Simmer for 15 minutes, stirring regularly
to ensure that the mixture doesn't catch on the bottom of the pan.

3 Remove from the heat and spoon into sterilised Kilner® Jars and seal
(pages 8 and 9). Store in a cool dark place for 1 week before using.
Once open, keep in the fridge and use within 1 month.

PLUM CHUTNEY

Makes 2 x 1 litre Kilner Jars

1kg plums, halved, stones
    removed and finely chopped
3 onions, peeled and finely
    chopped
100g dried cranberries or raisins,
    roughly chopped
1 tbsp finely grated fresh root
    ginger
1 tbsp black mustard seeds
1 tbsp ground cumin
1 tbsp paprika
1 tsp chilli flakes
750ml red wine vinegar
2 tbsp sea salt
500g light muscovado sugar

British plums can be used for creating a range of tasty recipes. Try making your own richly-spiced plum chutney from the recipe below.

1 In a Kilner® Preserving Pan, combine all of the ingredients apart from the salt and sugar and bring to the boil. Once boiling, reduce the heat, cover the pan and simmer for 10 minutes to tenderise the plums.

2 Add the sea salt and sugar and mix well to dissolve. Keeping the pan uncovered, boil the mixture for 25–30 minutes, stirring every so often to prevent it from sticking to the pan.

3 Transfer the chutney to sterilised Kilner® Jars and seal (pages 8 and 9). Leave to cool completely before labelling. Store in a cool dark place for at least 2 weeks to allow the flavours to mature before opening. Ideally, store for up to 6 months. Once open, keep in the fridge.

GINGERY BEETROOT CHUTNEY

This rich and flavoursome chutney is as good with cheese and biscuits as it is with curry. Once made, storing it for a few weeks allows the flavours to develop and improve, but if you really can't wait, go ahead!

1 Preheat the oven to 180°C/Gas 4. Meanwhile wash the beetroots. Place in an ovenproof dish, along with their stalks as they will give off their juices, and roast in the centre of the oven for 1½–2 hours depending on the size of the beetroot, until they are just starting to feel tender when pressed. Ideally they should not be completely cooked. Leave to cool before peeling.

2 Put the remaining ingredients apart from the crystallised ginger in a Kilner® Preserving Pan. Stir over a low heat to melt the sugar, then bring to the boil. Reduce the heat and simmer gently for an hour, stirring from time to time as the mixture thickens.

3 Chop the roasted beetroot into bite-sized chunks and add to the pan along with any juices from the roasting tin for the last 10 minutes. Taste and adjust the seasoning. Remove from the heat and leave to cool for 10 minutes before adding the crystallised ginger (if you add it immediately the ginger pieces will dissolve).

4 Spoon into sterilised Kilner® Jars, pressing the contents down, ensuring there are no air pockets, and then seal (pages 8 and 9). Leave to cool completely before labelling. Store in a cool, dark place for at least 2 weeks before opening. Once open, keep in the fridge and use within 2 months.

Makes 1 x 1.5 litre Kilner Jar

700g fresh beetroot, ideally with leaves on
3 onions, peeled and chopped
2 large cooking apples (Bramleys are good), peeled, cored and chopped
2 tbsp finely grated fresh root ginger
100g granulated sugar
250g muscovado sugar
1 tsp sea salt
650ml red wine vinegar
1 tsp ground allspice
3 cloves
100g crystallised ginger, chopped

JAMS, JELLIES & MARMALADES

Useful Equipment
Kilner Clip Top Jars and Bottles
Kilner Preserve Jars, lids
and seals
Kilner Jam Jar Tongs
Kilner Muslin Squares
Fine sieve
Kilner Jam Thermometer
Kilner Non-metallic Spatula
Kilner Waxed Paper Discs
Slotted spoon

MAKING YOUR FIRST PRESERVES: THE KILNER® METHOD

Making your own preserves is really rewarding as there are so many brilliant flavour combinations to experiment with. Once you're confident with your cooking skills, preserves can make the perfect homemade gift for anytime of year, from cozy Christmas presents to unique wedding favours stored in mini Kilner® Jars.

Step 1: Sterilising

Sterilise your jars following the methods on pages 8–9. Always sterilise more jars than you think you will need so that you are prepared if you produce more than expected.

Step 2: Prepare Your Recipe

Once you have selected your recipe, follow the instructions for preparation and making. Always read a recipe through a couple of times before you start making it so that you are familiar with the process and have all of the ingredients to hand.

Step 3: Fill the Jars

Once your recipe is ready, carefully remove your sterilised jars from the water bath or dishwasher, keeping them warm (pages 8 and 9). If they

Jam setting temperature

Using a Kilner® Jam Thermometer: When the thermometer reaches 105°C the jam should be set.

Using the 'wrinkle test': If you do not have a jam thermometer you can use this method. Place a plate in the freezer for around 15 minutes. Remove the jam from the heat and put a spoonful onto the cold plate. Allow it to set for a few seconds then push your finger gently into the jam. If the jam wrinkles and does not flood back into the gap, it is set.

contain any water, tip it away carefully. Always make sure you handle hot jars carefully – use Kilner® Jam Jar Tongs for protection.

Place the empty Kilner® Jars on a heatproof surface such as a chopping board and place a Kilner® Funnel, if using, in your first jar, then use a ladle to transfer your recipe from the pan to each of your Kilner® Jars making sure to fill them to within 1cm from the top.

Once each jar is filled use a non-metallic spatula to remove any air bubbles by running it around the inside of the jar (between the food and the jar).

Finally, wipe the rims and threads of the jar to remove any food debris.

Step 4: Sealing the Jars

Now your Kilner® Jars are filled, you need to close them while the contents are still hot.

If you are using a Kilner® Preserve Jar, place the discs onto your jars, add the screw-top band and tighten.

If you are using a Kilner® Clip Top Jar, place the rubber seals onto the top of the jar and close the clips. Place the jar in a large pan (ideally the Kilner® Preserving Pan) and cover the whole jar with water. Bring to the boil for 30 minutes. Once boiled, leave the water and jars to cool completely before removing. The process of boiling the jars in water adds extra heat to the contents, which allows a vacuum seal to form.

Step 5: Checking the Airtight Seal has Formed

Now that your jars are closed, you need to leave them to cool for 24 hours untouched.

After the 24-hour cooling period, check your jars to make sure an airtight seal has formed.

To check the seal of a **Kilner® Preserve Jar**, press the preserve disc with your finger. If the lid does not move then an airtight seal has formed but if the preserve disc pops up and down when pressed, an airtight seal has not formed and you must reprocess your jars or consume the contents immediately.

To check the seal of a **Kilner® Clip Top Jar**; undo the clip and lift the jar by the lid only. If an airtight seal has formed, the lid will not move. Now fasten, clip and store. If the lid moves, an airtight seal has not formed and you must reprocess your jars or consume the contents immediately.

Step 6: Storing Your Jars

Once the seals have formed, store your preserve jars in a cool, dry place for up to 6 months. Once the jars have been opened, only store your jars in the fridge and consume the contents within 2 weeks.

CHECKLIST FOR JAMS & MARMALADES

Preparation: Always use fresh, dry and slightly under-ripe fruit for best results. Only wash if necessary, and make sure you dry the fruit thoroughly afterwards.

Top tips: Simmering the fruit on its own before adding sugar or other ingredients will draw out the pectin and allow the fruit to soften. If using hard fruits, add a little water to the pan during stewing to help soften it.

If you prefer your fruit to remain whole or chunky, allow the sugar and fruit mixture to warm up gently before bringing to the boil.

Once your jam or marmalade has reached a rapid rolling boil, do not stir it as this may cause it to lose heat, and take longer to reach setting point.

Packing: Once setting point has been reached, allow the pan to rest for 10 minutes to give the mixture time to thicken a little more and encourage an even distribution of fruit. If the fruit rises to the top, stir the mixture to re-distribute it and pack immediately.

Storage: Store sealed jams and marmalades in a cool, dark, dry place and refrigerate once open, unless specified otherwise in the recipes.

CHECKLIST FOR JELLIES

Preparation: Soften the fruit thoroughly by simmering gently for 45–60 minutes.

Top tip: To achieve a clear jelly always strain it through a Kilner® Muslin Square that has been scaled in boiling water first, as this prevents the bag from soaking up the juices as you strain the jelly through it. Let the mixture strain through in its own time – forcing it through will cause a cloudy jelly.

Only add sugar once the mixture is boiling to keep it bright in colour. The longer you cook the sugar, the darker the jelly will be.

Packing: Transfer your finished jelly mixture to sterilised jars (page 8) as quickly as possible.

Do not leave the mixture standing in the pan.

Storage: Store sealed jellies in a cool, dark, dry place and refrigerate once open, unless specifed otherwise in the recipes.

APPLE & GINGER JELLY

Makes 4 x 0.25 litre Kilner Jars

900g cooking apples
  (Bramley are good), quartered
  (skins on)
2 lemons, quartered
70g fresh root ginger, peeled
  and chopped
1 cinnamon stick
4 cloves
1.5 litres cold water
About 450g preserving sugar
  for every 575ml liquid
  (see method)
Small knob of butter, optional
  (see method)

Tart and fresh, with just a hint of ginger, this is such a simple jelly but so versatile. Think roast pork, roast lamb, maybe a strong Cheddar cheese, smoked fish or just spread on a cracker!

1 Place the apples, lemons, chopped ginger, spices and cold water in a Kilner® Preserving Pan. Bring to a simmer, stirring from time to time, and cook for around 1 hour until the apples are mushy.

2 Pour the mixture into a Kilner® Muslin Square or fine sieve and leave to strain for at least 4 hours, ideally overnight. Do not press the mixture to speed things up as this will produce a cloudy jelly. Pour the strained juice back into the cleaned pan and bring to a simmer to reduce the liquid by about a third. Measure the resulting liquid and for each 575ml, add 450g preserving sugar.

3 Return the juice along with the preserving sugar back to the pan and bring slowly to the boil, stirring frequently to allow the sugar to dissolve. Turn up the heat and boil until setting point is reached, around 5 minutes – use a Kilner® Jam Thermometer or try the 'wrinkle test' (page 60). Remove any scum with a slotted spoon or disperse it by adding a small knob of butter.

4 Remove the pan from the heat and transfer the jelly to sterilised Kilner® Jars and seal (pages 60 and 61). Store in a cool, dry, dark place for up to 6 months. Once opened, store in a cool place and use within 1 month.

HOT PEPPER JELLY

This robust jelly is good with strong Cheddars or cold cuts. It also makes an ideal dipping sauce. You can adjust the quantity of chillies according to taste. Chillies are very low in pectin, hence the use of a cooking apple and a large quantity of preserving sugar.

Makes 2 x 0.25 litre Kilner Jars

1 dried chipotle or jalapeño chilli
5 red peppers, deseeded and finely chopped
65g mixed chillies, deseeded and finely chopped
1 large cooking apple (Bramleys are good), peeled
225ml cider vinegar
400g preserving sugar

1 Soak the dried chilli in boiling water for 2–3 minutes. Drain and when cool enough to handle, finely chop and along with any seeds, place in a Kilner® Preserving Pan. Add the chopped peppers and the mixed chillies.
2 Grate the apple, discarding the core. Add the flesh to the pan with the vinegar. Bring to a simmer and cook for about 2 minutes until the apple starts to break up, then add the preserving sugar. Stir and continue to simmer until the sugar has dissolved. Bring to a rolling boil for 3–4 minutes and then test for setting point (page 60).
3 Once setting point has been reached, remove the pan from the heat and transfer the jelly to sterilised Kilner® Jars (page 8) and seal (pages 60 and 61). When cold, store in a cool and dark place for up to 6 months. Once opened, keep in the fridge and use within 1 month.

> If you would like to label your jars once filled, make sure you leave them to cool completely first.

ORANGE JELLY
WITH LIME SHARDS

**Makes 1 x 0.5 litre
Kilner Jar**
10 thin-skinned oranges
Around 1.5 litres water
    (see method)
About 375g preserving sugar
    for every 500ml liquid
    (see method)
Juice and zest of 5 limes
4cm cinnamon stick

The proportion of jelly made to oranges used is small, so this is quite special and best made when oranges are plentiful and cheap. Use good-quality and thin-skinned ones. It is equally good on toast or served with smoked meats or fish – smoked mackerel in particular. A little goes a long way!

1 Wash the oranges and cut in half. Juice them (reserve the juice) and place the squeezed halves in a Kilner® Preserving Pan. Cover with water (you'll need around 1.5 litres). Simmer the orange halves for an hour or two until the skins are really soft.

2 Strain the liquid into a measuring jug along with the reserved orange juice. Discard the boiled orange halves. For every 500ml liquid, add 375g preserving sugar to the pan.

3 Add the lime juice and zest and the cinnamon stick. Stir well and bring slowly to a simmer to allow the sugar to dissolve before bringing to a rolling boil.

4 Continue to boil until setting point is reached (page 60). Allow to cool for 5 minutes before discarding the cinnamon stick and then transfer to sterilised Kilner® Jars and seal (pages 60 and 61). Store in a dark, dry and cool place for up to 6 months. Once opened, keep in the fridge and use within 1 month.

MINT JELLY

Makes 1 x 0.5 litre Kilner Jar

1kg cooking apples (Granny Smith are good), sliced, with skin and core
1 litre water
4 tbsp fresh lemon juice
Large bunch of mint
About 500g granulated sugar for every litre of liquid (see method)

The perfect partner to roast lamb.

1 Place the apple slices in a Kilner® Preserving Pan with the water, lemon juice and about 10 sprigs of mint. Bring to the boil and then simmer until a soft pulp is formed (about 30 minutes), stirring occasionally. Strain the mixture through a Kilner® Muslin Square or a sieve and allow to drip overnight.

2 Measure how much juice has been strained and work out the amount of sugar needed by using the calculation of 1 litre of liquid to 500g of sugar.

3 Transfer the prepared juice and sugar to a large heavy-based saucepan and bring to the boil. Finely chop 2 tablespoons of mint and add to the mixture.

4 Boil the mixture until a jelly forms. To test if the jelly is ready, turn the heat off the pan and spoon a few drops of jelly onto a saucer. Place the saucer in the freezer for a couple of minutes and if a jelly has formed when it is removed, then the mint jelly is ready.

5 Transfer the jelly to small sterilised Kilner® Jars and seal tightly (pages 60 and 61).

ROSEMARY JELLY

**This delicious jelly is the ideal accompaniment to roast pork
or lamb. Try adding a teaspoon to gravy for extra flavour too.**

1 Preheat the oven to 150°C/Gas 2. Strip the rosemary leaves from
their stalks. Reserve the stalks and scatter the leaves onto a baking sheet.
Place in the centre of the oven for 30–40 minutes to dry out. Remove
the dried leaves and set aside.

2 Put the chopped apples, together with their cores and pips, into a
Kilner® Preserving Pan. Pour in the water and add the reserved rosemary
stalks. Bring to the boil, then simmer gently, stirring occasionally, for
30–40 minutes or until the apples have turned to mush. Mash them
with a potato masher or fork.

3 Spoon the pulp into a Kilner® Muslin Square or a sieve and leave to
strain overnight. Measure the strained juice and calculate the sugar:
for every 600ml of juice use 450g of sugar (you should have about
1.2 litres of juice).

4 Put the strained juice, sugar, lemon juice and dried rosemary leaves
into a saucepan. Set over a moderate heat, stirring, until the sugar
has completely dissolved. Bring to the boil and cook at a rolling boil
for 20 minutes or until the jelly reaches the setting point (page 60).
Remove the pan from the heat while you test for a set.

5 Leave to cool for 10 minutes to ensure the rosemary is distributed
evenly. Ladle into warm sterilised Kilner® Jars, cover with waxed paper
discs and seal (pages 60 and 61). Store in a cool dark place for up to 9
months and refrigerate after opening. Once opened, use within 2 weeks.

Makes 2 x 1 litre Kilner Jars
Large handful of rosemary sprigs
900g sour cooking apples,
    roughly chopped
1.2 litres water
About 900g granulated sugar
    (see method)
Juice of 1 lemon

RHUBARB & GRAPEFRUIT JAM

**Makes 3 x 0.25 litre
Kilner Jars**
750g rhubarb, trimmed
    and cut into 1.5cm slices
Zest and juice of 2 large
    pink grapefruit
1 vanilla pod
750g preserving sugar

**Best made with the pale pink stems of forced spring rhubarb.
Rhubarb is very low in pectin so be sure to choose large, firm
(slightly under-ripe) grapefruit, if possible. We like to have this
as a soft set jam as it has such a beautiful colour and aroma,
which is lost the longer you cook it for.**

1 Put the sliced rhubarb, grapefruit zest and juice into a large glass or
china bowl (not metal).
2 With a sharp knife, slice open the vanilla pod and scrape out the seeds.
Add both pod and seeds to the bowl and stir well. Add the sugar, then
cover with a tea towel and leave for 24 hours.
3 Transfer the mixture to a Kilner® Preserving Pan and heat, stirring,
until the sugar has dissolved, before bringing to a fast rolling boil, skimming
the surface if needed, with a slotted spoon.
4 After 10 minutes, test the jam for setting point (page 60). Once the
setting point has been reached, turn off the heat and transfer to sterilised
Kilner® Jars, cover with waxed paper discs and seal (pages 60 and 61).

STRAWBERRY JAM

**Makes 1 x 0.35 litre
Kilner Jar**
900g fresh strawberries, rinsed
  and hulled
800g caster sugar
4 tbsp lemon juice

The easiest recipe ever for strawberry jam without using pectin!

1 Place the strawberries in a Kilner® Preserving Pan and crush with a potato masher or fork. Add the sugar and lemon juice. Stir over a low heat until all of the sugar has dissolved.
2 Increase the heat to high and and bring the mixture to a rolling boil. Continue to stir and boil until the mixture reaches 105°C.
3 Cool slightly, then transfer to hot sterilised Kilner® Jars, leaving about 1cm space below the lid, and seal (pages 60 and 61). The jam will keep for 6 months in a cool, dark place. Once opened, keep in the fridge.

BLUEBERRY & CHIA SEED JAM

Makes 1 x 0.5 litre Kilner Jar
375g blueberries
30g chia seeds
4 tsp stevia
Juice and zest of 1 lemon

This recipe features stevia, a sweetener and sugar substitute available from healthfood stores, and two superfoods: blueberries and chia seeds. Spoon the jam onto plain yoghurt or spread on toasted sourdough for a nutritious start to the day.

1 First, gently mash the blueberries to release the juices and form a thick purée. Place the chia seeds in a large bowl and mix in the stevia and blueberry purée. Cover and leave in the fridge for 2–3 hours. This will reconstitute the chia seeds so they're nice and plump.
2 Place the chia seed mixture in a blender and pulse until slightly smooth.
3 Sterilise a 0.5-litre Kilner® Clip Top Jar (see page 60). Pour the jam into the jar and seal (page 61).
4 Refrigerate and use within 4 days.

SWEET CHILLI JAM

Add a kick to fishcakes and salad or serve alongside cold cuts or cheeses.

1 Place the peppers, chillies (with seeds), ginger and garlic in the bowl of a food processor or blender. Whizz until finely chopped.
2 Transfer to a Kilner® Preserving Pan with the tomatoes, sugar and vinegar, then bring to the boil. Skim off any scum that comes to the surface with a slotted spoon, reduce the heat to a simmer and cook for 50 minutes, stirring occasionally.
3 Once the jam becomes sticky, continue cooking for 10–15 minutes, stirring frequently so it does not catch and burn. It should look like thick, bubbling lava. Cool slightly, transfer to sterilised Kilner® Jars, seal (pages 60 and 61). The jam will keep for up to 3 months in a cool, dark place. Refrigerate once opened and eat within 2 weeks.

Makes 1 x 0.5 litre Kilner Jar
8 red peppers, deseeded and
    roughly chopped
10 red chillies, roughly chopped
6cm piece of fresh root ginger,
    peeled and roughly chopped
8 garlic cloves, peeled
400g can cherry tomatoes
750g golden caster sugar
240ml red wine vinegar

PINEAPPLE & APRICOT JAM

**Makes 4 x 0.35 litre
Kilner Jars**
500g dried apricots
1.5 litres water
375g canned pineapple
Juice and finely grated zest of
   1 orange
Juice and finely grated zest of
   2 lemons
Juice of 3 limes
½ tsp cinnamon
850g preserving sugar

A delicious filling for a pavlova, an open tart, a Victoria sandwich cake or a fatless sponge. This jam is not reliant on seasonal fruits, so it can be made all year round. Add a handful of chopped pistachios or skinned almonds for additional crunch and colour, if liked.

1 Soak the dried apricots in the cold water for 24 hours. The next day, place the apricots and their soaking liquid in a Kilner® Preserving Pan and simmer gently for 45 minutes. Meanwhile, drain and chop the pineapple, reserving the juice.

2 Once the apricots are cooked, leave to cool and then cut into quarters or halves, according to your preference. Return to the pan along with any liquid that has collected on the chopping board.

3 Add the remaining ingredients, including the reserved pineapple juice, and bring slowly to the boil, stirring, until the sugar has dissolved. Boil for about 20 minutes, stirring from time to time until setting point is reached (page 60). If any of the fruit has caught on the base of the pan don't panic – it can take on the most delicious caramelised flavour, but be careful not to allow it to burn completely!

4 Once setting point has been reached, remove the pan from the heat and divide the jam between sterilised Kilner® Jars and then seal (pages 60 and 61). Store in a cool, dark place for up to 6 months. Once opened, store in the fridge and use within 1 month.

MIXED BERRY JAM
WITH STAR ANISE

Makes 2 x 0.5 litre Kilner Jars

1 kg bag frozen mixed berries
(such as blackberries,
redcurrants, blackcurrants
and raspberries)
3 star anise
1 kg granulated sugar

A berry jam that can be made at any time of the year. Most supermarkets sell bags of mixed frozen fruits for smoothie making but they're also excellent and economical to use in this easy-to-make, mixed berry jam.

1 Defrost the berries making sure you don't lose any of the juice that is created. Pour the fruit and juice into a Kilner® Preserving Pan and add the star anise. Bring gently to a simmer and cook until the fruit is fully softened.

2 Add the sugar and stir until it has dissolved, then boil rapidly until setting point is reached (page 60). Use a slotted spoon to remove the star anise and reserve. Divide the jam between sterilised Kilner® Jars and then top each jar with a star anise before sealing (pages 60 and 61). This is a nice surprise for whoever opens the jar, plus it will continue to flavour the jam.

PEACH & AMARETTO JAM

This recipe has no added pectin so it may not be as firm as store-bought jams but it is simply delicious served with toast, scones or pancakes.

1 Carefully peel the peaches using a vegetable peeler, or blanch briefly in boiling water, then remove the peel with a knife. Reserve the skins.
2 Halve and remove the stones from the fruit. Dice the flesh and place in a Kilner® Preserving Pan with the water and set aside for a moment. Place the skins in a small saucepan with enough water to cover, and boil until the liquid is reduced to 2 tablespoons.
3 Press the skins and liquid through a metal sieve into the peach flesh. Cover and simmer for 20 minutes, or until softened.
4 Add the lemon juice and warmed sugar to the pan. Heat, stirring, until the sugar has completely dissolved. Bring to the boil and cook for 10–15 minutes, or to setting point (page 60). Remove from the heat and skim any scum away from the surface using a slotted spoon.
5 Leave to cool for about 10 minutes, then stir in the amaretto liqueur. Transfer to warm sterilised Kilner® Jars and seal (pages 60 and 61). Store in a cool, dark place.

Makes 3 x 0.35 litre Kilner Jars
1.3kg peaches
250ml water
Juice of 2 lemons
1.3kg granulated sugar, warmed*
45ml amaretto liqueur

> * To warm the sugar, place it in an ovenproof container in
> a low-temperature oven (140°C/Gas1) for about 10 minutes.
> This helps the sugar melt when added to the jam pan.

APRICOT CURD

Makes 3 x 0.35 litre Kilner Jars

350g dried apricots
Juice and zest of 1 lemon
100g caster sugar
150g unsalted butter
4 large eggs

This delicate buttery curd is the perfect spread for bread and butter or try using it as a filling for meringues with a little whipped double cream.

1 Cover the apricots with cold water and soak overnight. The next day, simmer them gently in a Kilner® Preserving Pan with a well-fitting lid until they are really soft (around 1½–2 hours). You will need to check the pan from time to time in case the apricots are drying up; if so, add a little more water. Cool, then blitz in a food processor or blender until a smooth purée.

2 Place a heatproof mixing bowl over a saucepan of very gently simmering water, ensuring that the base of the bowl isn't touching the water. Add the apricot purée, lemon zest and juice, sugar and butter to the bowl and keep the water just below simmering. Stir constantly with a wooden spoon until the butter melts and the sugar dissolves.

3 In a separate bowl, beat the eggs well and then sieve into the apricot mixture, stirring all the time until the mixture becomes creamy and is thick enough to coat the back of a wooden spoon. Note: it will thicken more as it cools.

4 Remove the apricot curd from the heat. Pour carefully into sterilised Kilner® Jars and seal (pages 60 and 61). Store in the fridge and consume within 4–6 weeks.

LEMON CURD

Makes 2 x 0.35 litre Kilner Jars
3 large eggs, whisked
175g caster sugar
4 lemons (juice of 4, zest of 3)
125g unsalted butter, cubed

Homemade lemon curd is hugely satisfying to make and far tastier than the shop-bought variety. Essential to any lemon meringue pie, this zingy preserve also goes perfectly with toast.

1 Place the eggs, sugar, lemon juice and zest in a heatproof bowl and stir well before adding the butter.

2 Set the bowl over a heavy-based saucepan with 2.5cm of simmering water. It is important to make sure the bowl does not touch the water. Stir the mixture until the butter melts and then use a whisk to continually stir while it cooks for about 8 minutes or until it is thick enough to hold marks from the whisk.

3 Pour the lemon curd into sterilised Kilner® Jars and seal (pages 60 and 61). Keep in the fridge for up to 2 weeks.

ONION, PORT & THYME MARMALADE

This is a great fix that adds a real depth of flavour to sauces and gravies, as well as being a fine accompaniment to cold meats. Stir a little into onion gravy for the perfect treat with sausages and mash.

1 Heat the oil in a large pan, add the onions, salt and thyme and soften gently, stirring occasionally, for 15–20 minutes.

2 Once the onions are meltingly soft, add the remaining ingredients, including a good grind of black pepper, and bring slowly to the boil. Cook for a further 10 minutes or so, stirring occasionally, until most of the liquid has evaporated. Spoon the mixture into warm sterilised Kilner® Jars and seal (pages 60 and 61). The marmalade will keep for up to a year in a cool, dark place. Once open, refrigerate and use within 2 weeks.

Makes 2 x 0.35 litre Kilner Jars

4 tbsp olive oil

1kg onions, peeled, halved and thinly sliced

1 tsp sea salt

2 heaped tsp chopped fresh thyme leaves

110g dark brown soft sugar

3 tbsp balsamic vinegar

3 tbsp white wine vinegar

2 tbsp port

2 tbsp redcurrant jelly

Freshly ground black pepper

LIME & CRYSTALLISED GINGER MARMALADE

Makes 2 x 0.75 litre Kilner Jars
850g (about 12 limes)
2 litres water
1.7kg granulated sugar
100g crystallised ginger, chopped

Look out for thin-skinned limes, which are perfect for this marmalade. It's a real treat on thick buttered toast.

1 Rinse the limes, quarter them and then place in a Kilner® Preserving Pan with the cold water. Bring to the boil, then simmer for at least 2 hours, covered, to soften the peel.
2 Remove the limes with a slotted spoon and pour the liquid into a measuring jug. If necessary, top it up to a total of 1.5 litres with cold water.
3 When the fruit has cooled, cut it into bite-sized slices and return to the pan along with the cooking liquid and the sugar. Bring slowly to the boil, stirring, to dissolve the sugar. Once the sugar has dissolved, bring to a rolling boil and continue to boil until setting point is reached (page 60).
4 Remove from the heat and allow to rest for 10 minutes before adding the crystallised ginger. Stir well and then divide between sterilised Kilner® Jars and seal (pages 60 and 61). Store in a cool dark place for up to 6 months. Once opened store in the fridge and use within 1 month.

SEVILLE ORANGE MARMALADE

Makes 2 x 1 litre Kilner Jars
1kg Seville oranges
2.5 litres water
2kg demerara sugar
75ml lemon juice

Sticky, bittersweet Seville oranges are key to this classic marmalade.

1 Wash the oranges, then halve and juice them, reserving the squeezed halves. Slice the reserved halves into medium to thick pieces and place in a bowl along with the orange juice and the water. Leave to soak for 24 hours.

2 Transfer the mixture to a Kilner® Preserving Pan and bring to the boil. Reduce to a simmer and cook, covered, for 2 hours until the peel is soft and the marmalade has reduced. Add the sugar and lemon juice and mix well to dissolve the sugar.

3 Boil for about 20 minutes until setting point has been reached (page 60), then remove from the heat. Leave the marmalade to cool down for 10 minutes, then stir slowly to diffuse any foam from the top.

4 Pour the marmalade into warm sterilised Kilner® Jars and seal (pages 60 and 61). Store in a cool dark place for up to 2 years. Once opened, refrigerate.

OVERNIGHT OATS

3 GRAINS & NUTS

Serves 4
100g rolled oats
120g quinoa, cooked weight
200g raspberries, hulled
200g brown rice, cooked weight
600ml apple juice or milk of
    your choice
40g mixed nuts, toasted and
    roughly chopped

**This is such a versatile recipe so it is easy to make it your own.
Try using whatever wholegrain you have in stock, or just
use a different rice variety for each layer. Add the fruit, juice or
milk of your choice. You can even add a little honey or maple
syrup, do this before adding the liquid if you want to.**

1 Cook the quinoa and rice according to packet instructions, or use
pre-cooked packets.
2 Preheat the oven to 180°C/Gas 4. Take two baking sheets and
spread the oats out on them in a thin layer. Bake in the centre of the
oven for 8–10 minutes until lightly toasted, stirring halfway through.
Leave to cool.
3 Divide the cooled oats between sterilised Kilner® Jars (page 8),
followed by the quinoa, raspberries and rice. Pour over the apple
juice or milk and then finish with the nuts. Leave to soak and chill
overnight in the fridge. Store in the fridge for up to 3 days.
Best served at room temperature.

BANOFFEE PORRIDGE

Serves 4
450ml milk of your choice
100g rolled oats
A few pecan nuts, chopped
    in half
1 banana, peeled and sliced
Salted toffee sauce

If you are short on time, this recipe can be made in advance and stored in the fridge for up to 3 days until you are ready to grab and go.

1 Heat the milk gently in a small heavy-based saucepan. Add the oats and simmer while stirring frequently for 5 minutes. If the porridge becomes too thick, add a little more milk or water.

2 Meanwhile toast the pecan nuts in a dry frying pan for a couple of minutes.

3 Add half of the sliced banana and a swirl of salted toffee sauce to the porridge and stir. Ladle into sterilised Kilner® Jars (page 8) and top with more slices of banana, toasted pecans and add a swirl of salted toffee sauce to finish off. Eat straight away, or allow to cool and store in the fridge for up to 3 days.

SPICED APPLE BIRCHER MUESLI

This super-easy, super-delicious and healthy breakfast is ideal to make the night before, just add the toppings in the morning. Packed full of complex carbohydrates, fibre and healthy fats to keep you going throughout the day, this jar of goodness is sure to make breakfast that little bit more exciting.

You can make a larger batch of both the Bircher muesli and the apple topping (keep separately in the fridge) so you have breakfast ready for the week when time is short. Simply add the apples on top and take your Kilner® Jar to work, the gym – wherever!

1 The night before, mix together all of the Bircher muesli ingredients in your sterilised Kilner® Jar (page 8) and leave in the fridge overnight so the oats can soak everything up.

2 In the morning, chop the apple into chunks and place in a small heavy-based saucepan along with your chosen sweetener, the walnut pieces and cinnamon. Cook on a low heat for about 5–10 minutes until softened and slightly caramelised, then stir in the tahini and heat through, add to your muesli, and enjoy!

Serves 2

For the Bircher muesli
75g rolled oats
250ml almond milk
125g unsweetened apple purée
1 tsp vanilla extract
3 tsp sultanas
2 tbsp flaxseeds
1 tsp ground cinnamon
½ tsp mixed spice
Freshly grated nutmeg

For the apple topping
1 large apple (go for Braeburn
   or Pink Lady)
2 tbsp honey, maple syrup or
   coconut nectar
2 tbsp walnut pieces
½ tsp ground cinnamon
1 tbsp tahini

BREAKFAST APPLE CRUMBLE

Serves 4

1kg Bramley apples, cored
1 tbsp sunflower oil
4 drops of vanilla essence
1 tbsp honey
1 tbsp hot water
150g rolled oats
25g butter, chilled and diced
50g wholemeal flour
25g demerara sugar
1 tsp cold water
250g Greek yoghurt

This does take a bit of time but it is well worth the effort. It feels indulgent but with a reduced butter and sugar crumble plus all those oats and of course the apples, it really isn't as indulgent as it seems.

1 Preheat the oven to 180°C/Gas 4. Wrap the apples in kitchen foil and bake for about an hour until soft. Leave until fully cooled and then scoop out the flesh with a metal spoon, discarding the skins.
2 In a bowl, mix together the sunflower oil, vanilla essence, honey and hot water. Add the oats and stir thoroughly to combine, before spreading out over a baking sheet. Bake for 20–25 minutes until golden, stirring halfway through.
3 In another bowl, rub the butter and flour together, then stir in the sugar and a teaspoon of water – the mixture should be a bit lumpy! Sprinkle over a baking sheet and bake for 15–20 minutes until golden.
4 When everything is baked and fully cooled, start layering up sterilised Kilner® Jars (page 8). Sprinkle half of the oats between the bases of each jar, then top with baked apple followed by the Greek yoghurt, the remaining oats and finally the crumble. Best served at room temperature.

PEANUT BUTTER OATS

Serves 1, or multiply
quantities if you want
to make this in batches
for the week ahead.

**When there's no time to cook, overnight oats are the easiest way
to make a quick breakfast even quicker. Prepare for the week
ahead using these simple, healthy ingredients.**

For the overnight oats
45g rolled oats
1 tsp chia seeds
¼ tsp cinnamon
¼ tsp cocoa powder
¼ tsp vanilla extract
1 tsp honey (or your preferred
  sweetener)
2 tbsp peanut butter
120ml milk of your choice
  (almond, soy or dairy milk)

Suggested toppings
Chopped nuts of your choice
Dark chocolate shavings
  (70% or more)
Fresh fruit, chopped

1 Simply add the dry ingredients to enough sterilised Kilner® Jars for the
week ahead (page 8). Add the vanilla extract, honey, peanut butter and
milk the night before, then store in the fridge, allowing the oats to soak
up the liquid.
2 In the morning, just add your favourite toppings.

5

SALADS, SOUPS & LIGHT LUNCHES

Useful Equipment
Mixing bowl
Kilner Jars and Bottles
Kilner Spiralizer
Hand blender
Kilner Snack On The Go Jar
Blender or food processor

SPICED GRAINS

Makes 4 servings
4 tbsp mayonnaise
2½ tsp sriracha sauce
2 tbsp natural yoghurt
2 tbsp cold water
400g freekeh, ready cooked
200g edamame beans
200g quinoa, ready cooked
½ cucumber, deseeded and
   chopped
16 cherry tomatoes, halved
80g Cheddar cheese, grated
   (optional)
60g rocket

There are lots of grains that are easily available so if you have difficulty getting the freekeh (larger supermarkets stock it, or try your local health food store), just replace it with a different variety of rice or maybe some pearl barley.

1 Stir the mayonnaise, sriracha sauce, yoghurt and cold water together in a bowl and then divide between your sterilised Kilner® Jars (page 8).
2 Now add the remaining ingredients in the order in which they are listed here, finishing with the rocket. Seal (page 9) and chill in the fridge until ready to serve. This will keep in the fridge for 48 hours, but is best served at room temperature.

CLEMENTINE, CHICORY & PEANUT SALAD

A crisp and colourful winter salad, combining juicy clementines, crunchy chicory, tangy spring onions and peppery radishes, tossed in a spicy peanut dressing. This salad brings a healthy taste of summer to the dark winter months and is perfect served as a contrast to rich festive buffet food. It can also be made in advance: simply prepare the fruit and vegetables up to the end of Step 2, store the jars in the fridge until ready to serve and add the dressing, peanuts and chives at the last minute.

Makes 4 servings
4 clementines
4 spring onions
2 heads of chicory
6 radishes
125g peanuts (unsalted)
2 tbsp snipped fresh chives

For the peanut dressing
2 tbsp peanut butter
4 tbsp sunflower oil
2 tbsp white wine
1 tbsp white wine vinegar
1 tbsp light soy sauce

1 Peel the clementines and carefully remove any white membrane still clinging to them. Divide into segments and check that no white membrane remains. Divide between 4 sterilised Kilner® Jars (page 8).
2 Trim and slice the spring onions and add them to the jars. Remove the cores from the chicory heads and shred the leaves, adding them to the jars. Trim and quarter the radishes and add them to the jars.
3 To make the dressing, place all the ingredients in a Kilner Twist Top Jar and shake vigorously until well combined.
4 Pour the dressing over the salad in each of the jars and toss to combine. Scatter over the peanuts and chives. Serve immediately.

> **Variation**
> Replace the chicory with half a red cabbage, very finely shredded; replace the chives with 2 tablespoons of sultanas.

MEXICAN RICE & LIME

Makes 4 servings

3 tbsp lime juice
4 tbsp sunflower oil
1 tsp dried oregano
Pinch of sugar
1 tbsp cold water
Sea salt and freshly ground
    black pepper to taste
230g canned black beans
6 tbsp chopped fresh coriander
1 red chilli, deseeded and finely
    chopped
2 small avocados, diced
320g long grain rice
    (cooked weight), cooled
1 red pepper, deseeded
    and diced
250g canned sweetcorn
½ tsp chilli powder
A wedge of iceberg lettuce,
    shredded

This vibrant, tasty salad is perfect for lunch at your desk or make it in one large jar to take to a picnic – just turn out and toss to serve.

1 In a bowl, whisk together the lime juice, sunflower oil, oregano, sugar and cold water. Season and then divide between sterilised Kilner® Jars (page 8).

2 Add the black beans and then sprinkle over the coriander and chilli, followed by the avocados, rice, red pepper and sweetcorn. Sprinkle a little chilli powder into each jar and then top with iceberg lettuce. Seal (page 9) and chill in the fridge until ready to serve. This will keep in the fridge for 24 hours, but is best served at room temperature.

SIMPLE
SALADS
TO GRAB
AND GO!

Mango & Chilli Rainbow Fruit & Veg Salad

This energising lunch will see you through the busiest of days!

Serves 1, but simply multiply the quantities to make extra portions

1 mango, peeled, stone removed and chopped
½ fresh red chilli, deseeded
Squeeze of fresh lime juice
4 tbsp water
Sea salt and freshly ground black pepper to taste
¼ cucumber, chopped
1 carrot, grated
½ red pepper, deseeded and chopped
Handful of blueberries
4 radishes
Small handful of watercress

1 Take half of the prepared mango and add to a blender or food processor along with the chilli, lime juice and water. Season to taste and blend until smooth.

2 Add your required amount of dressing to the base of your freshly sterilised Kilner® Preserve Jar (page 8).

3 Layer the fruit and vegetables starting with the wettest ingredients first: mango, cucumber, carrot, red pepper, blueberries and radishes. Top with watercress sprigs. This will keep in the fridge for 24 hours, but is best served at room temperature.

Spanish Salad

Chorizo, a spicy pork sausage found throughout Spain and Portugal, is available smoked or unsmoked, mild or spicy and is sometimes flavoured with garlic or wine and always with smoked paprika. Here, it plays the starring role at lunchtime.

1 Layer your salad into a screw top jar and pour over the dressing just before serving. You can make up the salad in advance, seal (page 9) and chill in the fridge with the dressing in a separate container if you wish to save time – the Kilner® Snack on the Go Jar is perfect for this. This will keep in the fridge for 24 hours, but is best served at room temperature.

Serves 1, but simply multiply the quantities to make extra portions
50g chorizo, sliced
1 chargrilled red pepper, cut into pieces
1 carrot, thinly sliced or spiralised
Large handful of salad leaves (rocket and spinach work well)
Handful of black olives, pitted
Dressing of your choice (see page 20)

Prawn Satay Asian Noodle Salad

This salad is inspired by the delicious flavours of Southeast Asia.

1 Boil the fine egg noodles according to the packet instructions and leave to cool once cooked.
2 Place all of the dressing ingredients in a blender or food processor and blend until smooth. Add the required amount of dressing to a sterilised Kilner® Jar (page 8).
3 Add the cooled egg noodles to the jar and then layer with salad leaves and sweetcorn. Top with prawns and finish off with wedges of lime. Seal (page 9) and store in the fridge for up to 24 hours. Best served at room temperature.

Serves 2
250g fine egg noodles
1 little gem lettuce leaves
150g chopped baby sweetcorn
150g cooked tiger prawns
2 lime wedges

For the dressing
200ml coconut milk
Squeeze of fresh lime juice
120ml crunchy peanut butter
1 tbsp soy sauce
60ml vegetable oil
2–3 tbsp sweet chilli sauce
1–2 tbsp rice vinegar
½ tsp each of ginger and garlic purée

3 PEA & MINT SLAW

Makes 4 servings

200g sugar snaps, finely sliced
4 tbsp chopped fresh mint
   leaves
200g red cabbage, finely
   shredded
200g fresh peas
400g cooked chicken, shredded
200g mangetout, finely sliced

For the dressing

4 tbsp olive oil
2½ tbsp cider vinegar
1½ tsp Dijon mustard
Pinch of sugar
2 tbsp cold water
Sea salt and freshly ground
   black pepper to taste

This salad is really tasty and looks so fresh and pretty, plus with very little prep you don't need to spend long in the kitchen. It's a win-win!

1 To make the dressing whisk the oil, vinegar, mustard, sugar and cold water together, season and then pour into the dressing pot of the Kilner® Snack On The Go Jar.

2 Add the salad ingredients in the order in which they are listed into a Snack On The Go Jar, and chill until ready to serve.

ROASTED VEGETABLES WITH FETA

Makes 4 servings

1 large carrot (approximately 250g), peeled and chopped
1 large sweet potato (250g), peeled and diced
250g celeriac, peeled and diced
1 beetroot (approximately 250g), peeled and diced
5 tbsp olive oil
1 garlic clove, peeled and crushed
½ tsp chipotle paste
4 tsp sherry vinegar
2 tsp honey
2 tbsp water
230g cooked chickpeas
160g feta cheese, crumbled
60g baby spinach

Winter is often a time when salads are bypassed for something more substantial, but this combination of vegetables plus chickpeas will leave you feeling satisfied.

1 Preheat the oven to 200°C/Gas 6. In a bowl, toss the carrot, sweet potato, celeriac and beetroot with 1½ tablespoons of the oil, then tip onto a large baking sheet.

2 Arrange the vegetables in a single layer before roasting in the centre of the oven for 35–40 minutes until golden. Remove from the oven and leave to cool.

3 For the dressing, whisk the remaining oil with the garlic, chipotle paste, vinegar, honey and cold water. Divide the dressing between your sterilised Kilner® Jars (page 8), followed by the chickpeas. Add the cooled vegetables then the feta and finally top with spinach leaves. Seal (page 9) and store in the fridge. This salad can be made up to 3 days in advance. Best served at room temperature.

PEAR & STILTON WITH BALSAMIC VINAIGRETTE

Serves 1, but simply multiply the quantities to make extra portions
1 sunblush pear, cored and sliced
Handful of rocket leaves
Small handful of pomegranate seeds
Small handful of chopped pecan nuts
50g Stilton, chopped and cubed

For the balsamic vinaigrette
180ml extra virgin olive oil
60ml balsamic vinegar
½ tsp honey
Sea salt and freshly ground black pepper to taste

Here, the sublime combination of pears and Stilton cheese is enhanced by an aromatic balsamic dressing, pomegranate seeds, rocket leaves and pecans.

1 To make the dressing, add the olive oil, balsamic vinegar, honey and seasoning to a sterilised 250ml Kilner® Jar (page 8) and shake until throughly combined.
2 Add the desired amount of dressing to a sterilised 500ml Kilner® Preserve Jar (page 8).
3 Layer the salad ingredients, starting with the pear slices followed by the rocket leaves, pomegranate seeds and pecans, and top with Stilton cubes. This will keep in the fridge for 24 hours, but is best served at room temperature.

ROOTS & SEEDS LAYER

Makes 4 servings

5 tbsp sunflower seeds
5 tbsp pumpkin seeds
½ tsp oil
Sea salt and freshly ground
  black pepper
4 tbsp mayonnaise
1 tbsp yoghurt
1 tbsp wholegrain mustard
½ tsp white wine vinegar
1 tbsp cold water
250g swede, peeled and
  spiralised
12 rashers of streaky bacon,
  cooked, cooled and finely
  chopped
250g carrot, peeled and
  spiralised
2 spring onions, trimmed
  and finely sliced
60g lamb's lettuce

If you have only ever eaten swede cooked you will be surprised by its lovely peppery flavour and great crunchy texture.

1 Toss the seeds with the oil in a bowl and season with salt and pepper. Heat a large heavy-based frying pan until hot and then cook the seeds until lightly toasted. Shake the pan from time to time to prevent them burning. Tip onto a plate and leave to cool.
2 In another bowl, whisk together the mayonnaise, yoghurt, mustard, vinegar and cold water. Pour into the base of the sterilised Kilner® Jars (page 8) and then add the remaining ingredients in the order in which they are listed but adding the seeds before the lettuce. Seal (page 9) and chill in the fridge for up to 3 days until needed.

HOT & SOUR CHICKEN SOUP

Makes 4 x 0.5 litre Kilner Jars

1.6 litres organic chicken stock

1 chicken stock cube

2 tbsp tamarind concentrate

1 tbsp fish sauce

1 red chilli, deseeded and chopped

250g cooked chicken, shredded

1 large carrot (approximately 240g), spiralised

1 courgette (approximately 280g), peeled and spiralised

150g dried rice vermicelli

2 spring onions, trimmed and finely sliced

2 tbsp chopped fresh coriander

Juice of 1 lime

This soup is a perfect way to use up any leftover chicken from your Sunday roast. Alternatively, use prawns instead of chicken, or a combination of the two.

1 In a large heavy-based saucepan, heat the chicken stock until simmering. Add the stock cube, tamarind concentrate and fish sauce. Stir well to combine.

2 Add the remaining ingredients and cook for a further 3–4 minutes until piping hot and the vermicelli are cooked. Leave to cool completely before transferring to sterilised jars (page 8). Seal (page 9) and store in the fridge until ready to reheat. This soup will keep in the fridge for up to 3 days. Heat until piping hot before serving.

SPICED CARROT
& LEMON SOUP

A quick and easy carrot soup that packs a punch with the simple addition of ras-el-hanout. This North African spice mix is usually found in tagines but works equally well in this soup.

1 Heat the oil in a large heavy-based saucepan and add the onion. Cook over a moderate heat until softened. Add the carrots and cover with a well-fitting lid. Reduce the heat a little and continue to cook, shaking the pan from time to time for a further 10 minutes: the carrots should be softened but not browned.

2 Stir in the ras-el-hanout and cook for a minute before adding the stock. Bring to the boil and then reduce the heat to a gentle simmer and cook for 15 minutes.

3 Remove from the heat and use a hand blender to blend until smooth before transferring to sterilised Kilner® Jars (page 8). Add the lemon zest and juice, seal (page 9) and chill until ready to reheat.

Makes 4 x 0.5 litre Kilner Jars

1 tbsp olive oil
1 large onion, peeled and finely
   chopped
550g carrots, peeled and
   chopped
1 tbsp ras-el-hanout
1.2 litres vegetable stock
Juice and zest of 1 lemon

SWEET POTATO & CHIPOTLE SOUP

Makes 4 x 0.5 litre Kilner Jars

2 tbsp olive oil
1 large onion, peeled and finely chopped
1 large sweet potato (approximately 500g), peeled and chopped
1 tbsp chipotle paste
1.2 litres chicken stock
400g can black-eyed beans
200g sweetcorn
Juice of 1 lime
Tortilla chips to serve

This is more of a meal in a jar rather than just a soup! If you like things a bit more spicy, increase the amount of chipotle paste.

1 Heat the oil in a large heavy-based saucepan and then add the onion and cook until softened. Add the sweet potato and stir to coat in the oil and onion. Continue to cook for a further 5 minutes, covered with a well-fitting lid.

2 Add the chipotle paste, stirring well to combine, before pouring in the stock. Simmer gently for 15 minutes until the sweet potato is very soft, then blend with a hand blender until smooth. Add the beans, sweetcorn and lime juice before transferring to your Kilner® Jar (sterilise first, page 8). Seal (page 9) and store in the fridge until ready to reheat. Sprinkle the soup with tortilla chips to serve.

COCONUT MISO

Makes 2 x 0.35 litre Kilner Jars

1 sheet of dried egg noodles, cooked according to the packet instructions

2 carrots, peeled and grated

2 spring onions, trimmed and sliced

1cm fresh root ginger, finely chopped

50g broccoli, cut into florets

50g red cabbage, shredded

2 tbsp lemon juice

15ml tamari (or substitute soy sauce)

250ml coconut milk

6 tsp miso paste

1 tsp chilli paste

Handful of fresh bean sprouts

40g button mushrooms

Kilner® soups are quick and easy – the perfect answer for those who want fast food but like keeping it healthy. Taking nutritious lunches to work couldn't be any simpler and tastier with this recipe. Prepare the night before, seal and chill, then grab on your way out. All that's left to do is to add a little hot water to bring your jar back to life.

1 Divide the cooked noodles between the sterilised Kilner® Jars (page 8).

2 Add the carrots, spring onions, ginger, broccoli and red cabbage to a large heavy-based saucepan of boiling water. Blanch until just fork-tender. Remove from the heat and add the lemon juice, tamari (or soy sauce), coconut milk, miso paste and chilli paste. Stir well.

3 Divide the vegetables between the jars and top with fresh bean sprouts and mushrooms. Leave the water from the pan to cool and then add to the jars, filling only halfway up.

4 Seal your jars (page 9) and place in the fridge until ready to use. Add a little hot water to the jars to bring your spicy, fragrant soup back to life. Note: never pour boiling water directly into jars.

CHILLED MELON & GINGER SOUP

What could be more refreshing on a hot summer's day than a bowl of iced melon soup? The gingered cucumber relish in this recipe sets off the flavour of the melon to perfection.

1 Cut a very thin slice from the base of each melon so that it will stand upright. Then cut another slice about 2.5cm from the top. Place a metal sieve over a large bowl and, holding the melon over the sieve to catch any juices, scoop out and discard the seeds. Scoop out and reserve the flesh along with the juices.

2 Place the melon flesh (not juices) in a blender or food processor. Add the spring onions, ginger wine, dill and crème fraîche or yoghurt. Purée until smooth, then blend in up to 300ml of the reserved melon juice to give the required consistency. Season with salt and pepper, and add a little lime juice to taste. Divide between 4 sterilised Kilner® Jars (page 8), seal (page 9) and chill in the fridge for 1 hour.

3 Meanwhile, make the cucumber relish. Peel and halve the cucumber, scoop out the seeds and very thinly slice the flesh. Sprinkle with salt and set aside for 30 minutes.

4 Rinse the cucumber to remove the salt and pat dry on kitchen paper. Place in a bowl, stir in the remaining ingredients and season.

5 Top each portion of soup with a little cucumber relish. Drizzle over extra olive oil and serve garnished with dill sprigs.

Makes 4 x 0.35 litre Kilner Jars
4 small Charentais or Cantaloupe melons
4 spring onions, trimmed and finely chopped
60ml ginger wine
1 tbsp chopped fresh dill
150ml crème fraîche or Greek yoghurt
Sea salt and freshly ground black pepper
Lime juice to taste
Extra-virgin olive oil and dill sprigs to garnish

For the cucumber relish
125g cucumber
Sea salt and freshly ground black pepper
1 tbsp extra virgin olive oil
1 tsp lime juice
1 tbsp chopped fresh dill
1 tsp chopped preserved stem ginger, plus 1 tsp syrup from the jar

Variation
Add 225g cooked peeled prawns and process with the melon flesh, increasing the crème fraîche or yoghurt to 300ml.

SNACKS & DESSERTS

SPICED CHICKPEAS

Makes 1 x 0.5 litre Kilner Jar

2 x 400g cans chickpeas
2 tbsp olive oil
1 tsp ground cumin
1 tsp garlic powder
½ tsp chilli powder
½ tsp sea salt
¼ tsp freshly ground black
   pepper
Non-stick oil for spraying

This spicy chickpea mix is deliciously satisfying without too much salt or saturated fat.

1 Preheat the oven to 180°C/Gas 4.
2 Drain the chickpeas through a colander, rinse and thoroughly dry on kitchen paper. Place in a bowl with the olive oil, cumin, garlic powder, chilli powder, salt and pepper. With your hands toss well until the chickpeas are all evenly coated in the spicy mix.
3 Spray a rimmed baking sheet (or the chickpeas may escape) with non-stick oil and spread the chickpeas in a single layer, making sure not to overcrowd them. Roast in the oven, occasionally shaking the baking sheet to avoid them sticking, for 45 minutes or until nice and crunchy (check on them occasionally to make sure they do not burn).
4 Store the chickpeas in a sterilised Kilner® Jar (page 8) to keep them fresh and crunchy for up to 1 week.

MARINATED OLIVES & SPICED NUTS

Make these perfumed olives a month before Christmas to allow them to fully mature in flavour. The nuts can be made two weeks before the festive season begins. Serve with drinks or layer in small Kilner® Jars as gifts. They will last up to 2 weeks.

1 Using a rolling pin, lightly tap each black and green olive to split them without crushing completely, and remove the stones. Alternatively, slit with a small sharp knife. (Note: pitted olives do not need cracking.)
2 Arrange the black, green and stuffed olives in layers in a sterilised Kilner® Jar (page 8). Sprinkle each layer with coriander seeds and orange zest shreds. Tuck a few sprigs of coriander down the side of the jar.
3 Warm the olive oil in a heavy-based saucepan to release the aroma, then pour sufficient oil into the Kilner® Jar to cover the olives completely. Tapping the jar to release any air bubbles, seal tightly (page 9) and allow to cool. Leave in a cool dark place for up to 1 month to mature.
4 To prepare the nuts, preheat the oven to 150°C/Gas 2. Meanwhile, melt the butter in a roasting tin (or add the sunflower oil) and stir in the curry powder or garam masala. Cook, stirring, for 30 seconds. Add the nuts and seeds and stir with a wooden spoon until well coated.
5 Roast in the oven for 30 minutes, stirring from time to time – keep an eye on them as they can burn easily. On removal from the oven, immediately toss the nuts with the sea salt. Serve warm, or allow to cool completely and store in a sterilised Kilner® jar (page 8) for up to 2 weeks.

Makes 2 x 0.35 litre Kilner Jars

For the olives
200g each black, green and
    stuffed olives
2 tbsp coriander seeds
Finely pared zest of 1 orange,
    shredded
A few fresh coriander sprigs
450–750ml extra virgin olive oil
    (depending on the size of jar)

For the nuts
40g butter or 3 tbsp sunflower oil
1 tbsp curry powder or garam
    masala
350g mixed skinned nuts, such as
    almonds, pecans, hazelnuts
125g shelled mixed pumpkin and
    sunflower seeds
1 tsp coarse sea salt

PEANUT BUTTER FUDGE

**Makes 1 x 2 litre Kilner
Push Top Jar**
200g unsalted butter
250g smooth peanut butter
350g icing sugar
½ tsp sea salt

**This creamy delicious fudge is so quick and easy. Try making
a few batches to give to friends – present in Kilner® Jars
decorated with ribbons.**

1 Melt the butter and peanut butter together in a heavy-based
saucepan set over a medium heat. Gradually add the icing sugar,
stirring with a wooden spoon to incorporate. Finally, add the salt,
stirring, until fully combined.
2 Line an 18cm square baking tin with greaseproof paper and fill
with the mixture. Cover with more greaseproof paper and leave
in the fridge to set for 1 hour.
3 Cut into squares and enjoy!

ETON MESS

Serves 4
300ml crème fraîche
175g raspberries, hulled
3 meringue nests

For a special celebration, arrange this classic dessert in individual Kilner® Jars.

1 First, sterilise your Kilner® Jars (page 8) and allow to cool. Once cool, divide the crème fraîche evenly among the jars.
2 Top with a layer of raspberries. Break up the meringue nests and crumble over the top.
3 Close the lids to the jars and secure the clips. Chill in the fridge until you are ready to serve.
4 Just before serving, label tags with the names of each of your guests and add ribbon bows.

> **Variation**
> Swap the raspberries for your favourite berry, or whichever fruit is in season for a twist on this classic recipe.

GROUND COFFEE SYLLABUBS

Syllabub is a traditional English dessert of light and fluffy whipped cream. Freshly ground coffee gives this recipe a delightful speckled appearance and a lovely grainy texture.

Serves 6

125g caster sugar
300ml double cream
4 tbsp Kahlua or other coffee
   liqueur such as Tia Maria
2 tbsp finely ground coffee
4 tbsp water plus 4 tbsp ice-cold
   water
150ml whipping cream
2 tsp vanilla sugar
2 tbsp drinking chocolate
   powder

1 Place the caster sugar, double cream, coffee liqueur, coffee grounds and 4 tablespoons of water in a large mixing bowl. Whisk, using an electric beater or a balloon whisk, until the mixture is thick and floppy and holding a trail from the whisk.

2 Spoon or pour the syllabub mixture into small sterilised Kilner® Jars (page 8) – if you have one, pour the mixture through a wide-necked jam funnel to prevent the syllabub touching the sides of the glass as it goes in. Place the jars on a tray and set aside in a cool place for 2–3 hours, or chill in the fridge overnight.

3 Place the whipping cream in a large bowl with the vanilla sugar and 4 tablespoons of ice-cold water. Whisk, with an electric beater or a balloon whisk, until thick, light and frothy. Spoon the frothy cream on top of the syllabubs. Use a small metal sieve to dust with chocolate powder and chill until ready to serve.

> **Note:** If you replace the Kahlua with a less intense sweeter Tia Maria, use only 75g sugar.
>
>   If you make this syllabub the day before it is needed the cream and coffee will begin to separate out into two layers, which enhances, rather than detracts from the appearance.

NEAPOLITAN RIPPLE

Serves 4
175g strawberries, hulled
200g high-quality white chocolate
100g good-quality dark chocolate
75ml whole milk
284ml double cream
3 large egg whites
Pink food colouring, optional
White and dark chocolate shavings* and extra strawberry slices to garnish

White chocolate, dark chocolate and strawberries all in one jar! This is such a treat and looks great too. The quantities can easily be doubled.

1 Chop up the strawberries and place in a heavy-based saucepan. Cook over a gentle heat, mashing with a fork until soft and pulpy, then simmer for 1–2 minutes to thicken to a pulp. Remove from the heat.
2 Melt the white chocolate in a heatproof bowl set over a pan of gently simmering water (make sure the base of the bowl is not in contact with the water). Repeat with the dark chocolate.
3 Warm the milk until tepid. Now divide the melted white chocolate between two heatproof bowls and add half the warmed milk to one bowl and the blended strawberries to the other. Mix gently until fully combined. Add the remaining milk to the dark chocolate in another bowl and mix together.
4 Whisk the cream until it just holds its shape and then divide between the 3 bowls and fold in. Whisk the egg whites in another bowl until they form soft peaks and then fold into the 3 bowls until combined.
5 Spoon the 3 mixtures into sterilised Kilner® Jars (page 8), alternating to achieve a layered effect. Chill in the fridge until ready to serve, garnished with white and dark chocolate curls and strawberry slices.

> * To make the chocolate shavings, either grate the chocolate on the largest side of your grater or run a vegetable peeler along the edge of the chocolate several times.

CHOCOLATE MOUSSE

Serves 4

70g dark chocolate, plus extra
  finely chopped chocolate
  to garnish
½ tsp unsalted butter
¼ tsp instant coffee powder
1 egg, separated
Chopped nuts to garnish,
  optional

Rich, dark chocolate mousse – the perfect finale to any dinner party.

1 First, break up the chocolate into squares and place in a heatproof bowl. Set the bowl over a heavy-based saucepan containing roughly 2.5cm of simmering water. It is important to make sure the bowl does not touch the water.

2 Add the butter and melt with the chocolate, stirring frequently, then sprinkle in the instant coffee powder. Remove from the heat and allow to cool for 2–3 minutes. Add in the egg yolk and beat together until a smooth consistency is reached.

3 In another bowl, beat the egg white until stiff peaks are formed. Gently fold the egg white into the chocolate mixture using a metal spoon.

4 Spoon the mousse evenly between the sterilised Kilner® Jars (page 8), then sprinkle with finely chopped chocolate and chopped nuts, if using. Close the lids and secure the clips. Chill in the fridge for at least 2 hours or until ready to serve.

FRUIT SALAD WITH PISTACHIO BISCUITS

Crisp, pistachio nut biscuits make a great accompaniment to this refreshing dessert. The recipe makes 18 – store the rest in a Kilner® Clip Top Jar to keep them crisp.

1 First, make the biscuits. Preheat the oven to 200°C/Gas 6. Line a baking sheet with greaseproof paper and grease 2 or 3 rolling pins.
2 Cream the butter and sugar together in a mixing bowl, until very light and fluffy. Sift in the flour and mix well, then add the milk and beat until smooth. Stir in the pistachio nuts.
3 Place 6 teaspoonfuls of the mixture on the baking sheet, spacing them well apart. Bake for 5–7 minutes until golden brown around the edges. Leave to firm up slightly for about 30 seconds, then lift off using a palette knife and place over a rolling pin, pressing gently for a few seconds to curve. When firm, lift off the biscuits and transfer to a wire rack to cool. Bake the remaining mixture in the same way.
4 For the syrup, place the sugar in a small heavy-based saucepan with the water and dissolve over a low heat, stirring occasionally. Increase the heat and bring to the boil. Boil rapidly for 2 minutes, then remove from the heat and stir in the orange juice and liqueur, if using.
5 Working on a plate to catch the juices, remove the peel and white pith from the oranges using a sharp knife, then cut out the segments. Halve and remove the stones from the plums, apricots and peaches, then cut into thick wedges. Place the fruits into 4 individual small Kilner® Jars (sterilise first, page 8), together with any juice, and pour over the warm syrup. Chill in the fridge for up to 2 hours.
6 To finish, stir in the redcurrants and raspberries. Serve at once, accompanied by 2–3 pistachio biscuits per person, and some thick pouring cream if desired.

Serves 4
2 oranges
5 plums
4 apricots
2 peaches
125g redcurrants, hulled
125g raspberries, hulled
Thick pouring cream to serve

For the syrup
25g caster sugar
100ml water
300ml orange juice
1–2 tbsp eau de framboise (raspberry liqueur), Grand Marnier or crème de cassis (optional)

For the pistachio biscuits
75g shelled pistachio nuts, finely chopped
75g unsalted butter (at room temperature)
125g caster sugar
50g plain flour
2 tbsp milk

MIX & BAKE CHOCOLATE, WALNUT & OAT COOKIES

Makes 25 cookies (using a 1.5-litre Kilner Jar)

250g plain flour
¾ tsp baking powder
250g dark brown soft sugar
100g rolled oats
100g caster sugar
200g dark chocolate chips
100g walnuts, roughly chopped

The perfect gift for someone who loves to bake or is just learning. Or keep a jar made up ready for unexpected guests. With this easy-to-follow method you will soon be eating freshly baked cookies with minimal effort.

1 Sift the flour and baking powder together in a bowl then transfer to a 1.5-litre Kilner® Jar. Tap the base gently to level the mixture then add the remaining ingredients in the order in which they are listed.
2 Write out or print out a label with the cooking instructions as follows:

Preheat the oven to 180°C/Gas 4. In a bowl beat 250g softened butter, 1 large egg and 1 teaspoon of vanilla essence until light and creamy. Add the contents of the jar and mix together well. Place heaped teaspoonfuls of the mixture on 2 large greased baking sheets, allowing space for each cookie to spread as they cook. Bake in the centre of the oven for 12–15 minutes. Leave to cool on the baking sheets for 5 minutes before transferring to a wire rack to cool fully. Store in an airtight container for up to 1 week.

Add butter + egg + bake at 180C/gas 4, 12–15 minutes.

ROCKY ROAD POPCORN PIECES

Makes enough to fill a 1 litre Kilner Jar
50g salted butter
70g popcorn kernels
60g milk chocolate, melted
 (page 128)
65g mini marshmallows
65g malted chocolate balls

Great for snacking, these delicious bites also make a delightful gift for family and friends!

1 Melt the butter in a large, deep saucepan with a tight-fitting lid. Add the popcorn kernels and stir with a wooden spoon to ensure each one is coated in butter. Turn the heat down to low and place the lid on the pan. Leave to cook until you hear popping, gently shake to prevent kernels from burning but do not remove the lid from the pan.
2 When you hear the popping sounds begin to slow down, hold the lid down and shake the pan gently to avoid the popcorn burning at the base of the pan. Remove from the heat and leave the lid on for a few minutes.
3 Spread the popcorn out onto a baking sheet and drizzle with melted chocolate. Finish off by sprinkling with marshmallows and malted chocolate balls. Leave to set. Cut into bite-sized pieces using a sharp knife and store in sterilised Kilner® Jars (page 8) for up to 1 week.

BOTTLED SPICED PEARS, PEACHES & NECTARINES

Beautiful bottled fruits, picked in their prime and poached in a sweet-sour and spiced sugar syrup, make a delightful gift. Use whole spices for optimum flavour and effect.

1 Carefully peel the pears – avoid using over-ripe fruit or it will discolour and disintegrate during cooking. Halve or quarter, then remove the cores. Place in a bowl of water with a little vinegar added to prevent discolouration.

2 Thinly slice the ginger and pare the zest from the lemon in a single strip. Place the sugar and vinegars in a large heavy-based saucepan and dissolve the sugar over a gentle heat. Once dissolved, add the ginger, lemon zest, spices and drained pears. Slowly bring to the boil and simmer gently for about 20 minutes or until the pears are just tender – they must remain whole.

3 Lift out the pears with a slotted spoon and pack into sterilised Kilner® Bottles (page 8), with an even distribution of the cooked spices.

4 Bring the cooking liquid to the boil and then simmer for 10 minutes or until syrupy. Pour over the pears, making sure the syrup is evenly distributed. Seal (page 9) and store in a cool dark place for up to 6 months.

Makes 1 x 1 litre Kilner Bottle
900g ripe but firm, unblemished pears
2.5cm piece of fresh root ginger
1 lemon
450g golden granulated sugar
300ml white wine vinegar
300ml clear malt vinegar
1 tbsp allspice berries
1 tbsp cloves
1 large cinnamon stick

> **Variations**
> For spiced peaches or nectarines, prepare in exactly the same way but skin, halve and remove the stones from the fruit. Use orange instead of lemon zest and omit the ginger.

7

DRINKS

Useful Equipment

Kilner Cocktail Shaker
Kilner Handled Jars
Kilner Jars and Bottles
Muddler/wooden spoon
Food processor/blender
Pestle and mortar
Kilner Muslin Squares
Kilner Funnel
Slotted spoon
Kilner Jam Thermometer
Kilner Juicer

LONG ISLAND ICED TEA

Serves 2
Ice cubes
25ml vodka
25ml gin
25ml gold tequila
25ml light rum
25ml Cointreau
Juice of 1 lemon
35ml simple syrup*
Coca-Cola, orange slices
　　and ice, to serve

There are no special techniques needed for this cocktail – just make sure you have plenty of ice!

1 Half-fill your Kilner® Cocktail Shaker with ice and add all the spirits along with the lemon juice and simple syrup. Screw on the lid and shake well to mix.
2 Half-fill your Kilner® Handled Jars with ice and strain the cocktail into them. Top up with Coca-Cola and serve garnished with orange slices.

* Simple syrup is made by dissolving water and sugar together in equal quantities. Heat gently, stirring until the sugar has dissolved then cool and store until ready to use.

CRANBERRY MARTINI

This variation on a classic Martini is the ideal signature cocktail for any festival gathering.

1 Half fill your Kilner® Cocktail Shaker with ice and add the vodka, vermouth and cranberry juice. Screw on the lid and shake vigorously up and down for about 10 seconds. Strain into glasses, dividing evenly.
2 Garnish each glass with 2 frozen cranberries and a lemon zest twist. Serve immediately.

Serves 4
Ice cubes
240ml vodka
60ml dry vermouth
120ml cranberry juice
8 frozen cranberries
4 lemon zest twists*

* How to make a lemon zest twist: use a vegetable peeler to remove a wide strip of zest, with as little pith as possible. Twist the peel into a more curled shape if desired – it should hold after a few seconds.

BLUEBERRY & GRAPEFRUIT SPRITZER

Serves 1
40g blueberries
3 fresh mint leaves
1 tbsp fresh lime juice
2 tbsp ice
Grapefruit soda, chilled

For an extra-special fizz replace the soda with a sparkling cava or prosecco.

1 In a Kilner® Handled Jar, place the blueberries and fresh mint. Using a muddler or wooden spoon, crush together to release the flavours and essential oils from the mint. Add the fresh lime juice, ice and top with grapefruit soda.
2 Screw the Kilner® Cocktail Shaker lid onto the jar, followed by the top. Shake thoroughly to mix. Remove the lid and pour directly into a Kilner® Handled Jar.

KIWI & BLUEBERRY MOJITO

Serves 4
5 kiwi fruit, peeled and cut in half
100g granulated sugar, plus extra to garnish
300ml lime juice
150–250ml rum
Ice as needed
Handful of mint leaves
5 kiwi fruit, peeled and sliced
120g blueberries, crushed (use a muddler or wooden spoon for this, see above recipe)
120g whole blueberries
350–475ml sparkling water

The mojitos can be served in a Kilner® Clip Top Bottle, Kilner® Handled Jars, or in a Kilner® Cocktail Shaker.

1 Put the kiwis in a food processor with the granulated sugar and lime juice. Pulse until you have a coarse purée. Now add the rum – start with the lower amount and adjust as you prepare the drink.
2 To make a pitcher, pour the kiwi purée into a cocktail jug and add a layer of ice, a good amount of mint leaves and kiwi slices. Next, add a few more ice cubes, the crushed blueberries, some more mint leaves and the whole blueberries. Top off with sparkling water and stir gently. Taste and add more rum, sparkling water, or sugar if needed.
3 To make in individual Kilner® Handled Jars, follow the steps above but add a few whole blueberries at the beginning.

HOMEMADE SPICED GIN

Makes 400ml
1 tbsp juniper berries
400ml good-quality gin
A few fennel seeds
A few small pieces of crushed
 whole allspice
1 tsp coriander seeds
2 cardamom pods
2 whole peppercorns
1 torn bay leaf

Optional flavourings
Small sprig each of lavender
 and rosemary
Small strip of grapefruit peel
Small piece of unwaxed lemon

Create your own bespoke gin at home with our easy-to-follow recipe.

1 Ensure the Kilner® Bottles are sterilised (page 8).
2 In a pestle and mortar, crush the juniper berries a little to help release the aromatics and then place them inside the sterilised bottles. Pour over the gin and seal (page 9). Leave for 12 hours in a cool, dark place.
3 Taste your gin. It will now taste of the junipers and be taking on the characteristics of gin. If you prefer a stronger flavour, add more juniper berries and leave for a further 12 hours. Once you are happy with the level of juniper, strain the gin through a metal sieve into a jug to remove the junipers.
4 Divide the remaining herbs and spices (and optional flavourings if desired) between the Kilner® Bottles and top up with the juniper-infused gin. Close the bottles and leave for a further 36 hours, shaking often.
5 Filter the gin using the funnel, lined with Kilner® Muslin Squares to remove the herbs and spices and then return the gin to the bottles and label. The gin can be stored for up to 12 months in a cool, dry place.

CRANBERRY GIN

Surprisingly simple but oh so delicious!

1 Prick the skin of the cranberries with a small knife to allow the juice to pour out during the infusing process.

2 Transfer the cranberries, caster sugar and gin to a sterilised 1-litre Kilner® Clip Top Jar (page 8). Close the lid and shake well to thoroughly combine all of the ingredients. Allow the mixture to infuse for a week in a cool, dark place, shaking twice a day.

3 Decant the gin into freshly sterilised (page 8) 250ml Kilner® Clip Top Bottles and serve with tonic and ice.

Makes 500ml
100g cranberries
100g caster sugar
500ml of a gin of your choice
    (or make your own, page 140)
Tonic and ice to serve

GRAPEFRUIT GIN FIZZ

Grapefruit juice, gin and Campari make a refreshing combination on a hot summer's day.

1 Stir the grapefruit juice, soda water, gin and Campari together in a cocktail jug.

2 Fill 4 Kilner® Handled Jars with ice and top with the cocktail mixture. Garnish with grapefruit wedges and serve.

Serves 4
400ml red or pink grapefruit
    juice, preferably freshly
    squeezed
400ml soda water
125ml gin
2 tbsp Campari
Ice cubes
Grapefruit wedges to garnish

POMEGRANATE VODKA

Makes 1 x 1 litre Kilner Bottle

75cl premium vodka (preferably 35% ABV)
1 large pomegranate (seeds only)
Handful of raspberries
210g caster sugar

Here, vodka is given an exotic twist with the addition of pomegranates.

1 Mix all the ingredients together in a jug.
2 Add your mix to a sterilised Kilner® Clip Top bottle (page 8) and leave to infuse for 2 weeks in a cool, dark place, shaking each day.
3 Serve as shots in a unique and fashionable way by using our Kilner® Mini Jars.

CHAI-SPICED VODKA

Makes 1 x 0.55 litre Kilner Bottle

3–4 cardamon pods, lightly crushed with the green outer skins
4–5 peppercorns, barely crushed
5–6 cloves
2.5cm piece of cinnamon, broken up into small pieces
Small piece of dried ginger, broken into tiny pieces
400ml good-quality unflavoured vodka

Inspired by Chai-spiced tea, this aromatic vodka is wonderfully warming.

1 Add all of the spices to a sterilised Kilner® Clip top bottle (page 8).
2 Using a funnel, gently decant the vodka into the bottle, filling it up to the neck. Seal (page 9) and allow to steep in a cool, dark place for 1 month.
3 Feel free to strain out the spices after a month using a funnel lined with muslin squares, or a small sieve, or just leave them in for a more intense flavour.

SPICED APPLE COCKTAIL

Aromatic gin, ginger beer, lemon juice, cinnamon and sugar perk up apple juice perfectly!

1 Add the gin, apple juice, ginger beer, lemon juice, cinnamon and sugar to a Kilner® Cocktail Shaker.
2 Screw the cocktail shaker top onto the jar followed by the lid. Shake thoroughly to mix all the ingredients together.
3 When you're happy the mixture has blended, remove the cap and pour into a Kilner® Handled Jar. Garnish with apple and lemon slices and lots of ice.

Serves 4
350ml dry gin
280ml apple juice
280ml ginger beer
7 tsp lemon juice
2 tsp ground cinnamon
2 tsp granulated sugar
Apple and lemon slices
    and ice to serve

SMOKY BLOODY MARY

Serves 1
Ice cubes, plus extra to serve
50ml vodka
100ml tomato juice
2–3 dashes of chipotle Tabasco
Pinch of smoked paprika
2 dashes of Worcestershire
    sauce
Pinch of celery salt
Pinch of black pepper
Juice of ¼ lemon
Celery stick to garnish

This is the perfect accompaniment to a long, lazy brunch. Adjust the Tabasco according to taste.

1 Half-fill your Kilner® Cocktail Shaker with ice. Add all the ingredients apart from the celery, screw on the lid and shake well to mix.
2 Strain into a Kilner® Handled Jar, half-filled with ice, and serve garnished with a celery stick.

PIÑA COLADA

Serves 2
400g can coconut milk,
½ medium pineapple,
    cut into chunks
Splash of light rum
Ice

This cocktail will have you dreaming of tropical beaches – fresh pineapple juice, coconut milk and a splash of light rum – pure heaven!

1 Set the pineapple on a chopping board and lay it on its side. Turn the pineapple to remove the top and the leaves with a sharp knife. Starting at the top, slice through the outside peel until you reach the bottom on all sides. Quarter the pineapple and remove the core.
2 Juice the pineapple in a juicer or high-powered blender and mix with the coconut milk. Add a splash of light rum and serve in Kilner® Handled Jars over ice.

HOMEMADE TONIC WATER

Makes 2 x 0.25 litre
Kilner bottles
Juice and zest of ½ orange
Juice and zest of ½ lemon
Juice and zest of ½ lime
3–4 small pieces of lemongrass
14g cut cinchona bark (available
  online)
½–1 tbsp additional herbs and
  spices, optional (coriander
  seed, cardamom, juniper,
  allspice all work well)
200ml water
200g natural cane sugar
15g citric acid (from chemists
  and some homeware stores)
Pinch of salt

Traditionally used as a natural protection against malaria due to its quinine content, tonic water is now hugely popular across the globe as the perfect partner for gin. This recipe uses natural ingredients for a fresh and zesty flavour.

1 Ensure the bottles are sterilised (page 8).
2 Use a sharp knife to remove the zest in large strips from the citrus fruits (leave the white pith behind) and then juice the fruits. Slice the zest into small pieces. Divide the juice and zest between the Kilner® Bottles.
3 Divide the lemongrass, cinchona bark, optional extra herbs and spices and 100ml of the water between the bottles. Seal (page 9) and refrigerate for 3 days, shaking intermittently.
4 Meanwhile, make the simple syrup by combining the remaining 100ml water with the sugar in a medium-size saucepan. Bring the mixture to a simmer over a medium–low heat until the sugar has dissolved.
5 Remove the saucepan from the heat and whisk in the citric acid and salt. Allow to cool to room temperature and chill until the cinchona mixture has finished steeping.
6 After 72 hours, strain the cinchona mixture using a funnel lined with muslin squares. Whisk the simple syrup into the cinchona mixture until thoroughly combined.
7 Transfer the tonic concentrate back to the bottles and store in the fridge for up to 2 months.
8 To dilute and serve, combine tonic concentrate with plain soda water (experiment with 1 part tonic to 1 part soda or up to 2 parts soda).

PINK LEMONADE

The prettiest and most delicious taste of summer!

1 Place all the ingredients in a heavy-based saucepan and pour over the cold water. Bring to the boil, stirring frequently, then leave to cool.
2 Strain through a sieve into a sterilised Kilner® Preserve Jar (page 8), pressing down with a metal spoon to extract all the juices. The syrup can now be stored in the fridge for up to 1 week.
3 To serve, pour a little lemonade into a glass tumbler and top up with sparkling or still water, ice and mint sprigs.

Makes 350ml syrup
300g caster sugar
1½ lemons, sliced
1 orange, sliced
3 x 170g punnets raspberries
350ml cold water
Sparkling or still water, ice and
    fresh mint to serve

LEMON CORDIAL

Serve with iced water for a summertime refresher.

1 Scrub the lemons and pare the zest from 4 of them. Bring a Kilner® Preserving Pan of water to the boil, then drop in all the lemons for 1 minute. This will soften them and they will give more juice.
2 Use a slotted spoon to lift out the lemons reserving the lemon-infused water. Squeeze the juice from the lemons and measure 500ml.
3 Put the sugar, lemon zest and 500ml of lemony water into a large heavy-based saucepan. Heat gently to dissolve the sugar, then bring to the boil. Add the 500ml of lemon juice and bring just to boiling point. Remove from the heat and strain through a sieve into a jug. Transfer immediately to hot, sterilised Kilner® Bottles and seal at once with the swing-top lid (pages 8 and 9).
4 Leave to cool, then store in a cool, dry place or in the fridge for up to 4 months. To serve, mix one part syrup to four parts water.

Makes 1 x 1 litre
Kilner Bottle
7–10 unwaxed lemons
650g granulated sugar

GINGER & LEMON CORDIAL

Makes 350ml
350g fresh root ginger (peeled
    weight approximately 275g)
Juice of 4 lemons
200g caster sugar

This delicious cordial is a perfect winter warmer, served hot or cold. Use big pieces of fresh root ginger as they are the juiciest!

1 Peel and roughly chop the ginger and then place in a blender or food processor along with the lemon juice. Pulse until the ginger is puréed (you may need to add a little water if the mixture is too thick).
2 Tip the mixture into a glass mixing bowl, add the sugar and stir well. Cover with a tea towel and set to one side for 30 minutes.
3 Strain the mixture through a Kilner® Muslin Square or a fine nylon sieve, pressing the mixture firmly to extract as much cordial as possible. Store the cordial in a Kilner® Clip Top Bottle and serve diluted with still or sparkling water, over ice.

PEACH CORDIAL

**Makes 1 x 1 litre
Kilner Bottle**
2 vanilla pods
1 kg peaches
250g granulated sugar
Juice of 1 lemon
Juice of 1 lime

The delicate taste of peaches captures perfectly the essence of summer.

1 Slice the vanilla pods in half and scrape out the seeds. Wash the peaches in cold water, cut them in half and remove stones.
2 Place the peaches (skins included) into a food processer and blend to a puree.
3 Add the peach puree to a Kilner® Preserving Pan with the vanilla seeds, sugar and a squeeze of lemon and lime juice. Stir everything together.
4 Heat gently to dissolve the sugar and simmer for 15 – 20 minutes until thickened.
5 Using a Kilner® Funnel, pour into sterilised Kilner® Bottles (page 8). Seal at once with the swing top lid (page 9).
6 Leave to cool, then store in a cool, dry place or in the fridge for up to 4 months. To serve, mix one part syrup to four parts water.

ALMOND MILK

Almond milk has a delicious creamy nutty taste, making it perfect for use in overnight oats, poured over delicious crunchy granola, or for a delicious dairy-free hot chocolate. This recipe requires you to soak almonds overnight, but it's worth the wait!

Makes around 1.5 litres
175g raw unsalted almonds
½ tsp salt
1½-litres water
4 pitted Medjool dates
2 scraped vanilla beans

1 Place the almonds, salt and 500ml of water, in a medium-size bowl. Soak the almonds overnight.
2 After the soaking period is complete, drain the water and rinse the almonds. Squeeze the almonds to remove the skin.
3 Place the almonds, the remaining water, dates and scraped vanilla beans into the blender. Blend everything together for 60 seconds on high.
4 Strain the milk through a nut bag/Kilner® Muslin Square or tea towel into a jug or bowl, by slowly squeezing the bag like you're milking a cow.
5 Using a jug or a funnel, pour the milk into a Kilner® Clip Top Bottle and use within 7 days.

CARROT, APPLE & TURMERIC JUICE

Serves 2

2 large carrots, trimmed
(approximately 300g)
1 large eating apple, cored and
roughly chopped
2.5cm piece of fresh turmeric,
peeled and roughly chopped
½ tsp coconut oil
Pinch of black pepper
2 tbsp boiling water
Juice of 1 grapefruit
Ice, optional

This super-healthy juice is a perfect way to start the day. Coconut oil and black pepper along with the hot water are important additions to help fully activate the benefits of the turmeric.

1 Juice the carrots and then pour into a blender. Add the apple and turmeric and pulse until smooth.
2 Stir the coconut oil and black pepper into the boiling water, then add to the blender along with the grapefruit juice. Pulse until mixed. Pour into a Kilner® Handled Jar and serve, adding ice if preferred.

SUNSET SMOOTHIE

Serves 1–2
2 blood oranges
½ medium pineapple
Ice, to serve

This is a real fruity number! You could add a dash of tequila to make it a perfect sunset, but if you're going for the healthy option, it is equally good without alcohol. Blood oranges are great for juicing and also high in antioxidants.

1 First, peel the oranges, leaving as much of the white pith as possible. Now juice the oranges, transfer to a jug and leave to chill in the fridge.
2 Set the pineapple on a chopping board and lay it on its side. Turn the pineapple to remove the top and leaves with a sharp knife. Starting at the top, slice through the outside peel until you reach the bottom on all sides. Quarter the pineapple and remove the core.
3 Place the pineapple pieces in a blender with a handful of ice, then process until smooth.
4 Pour the orange juice into a Kilner® Handled Jar and top up with the thick pineapple juice. Mix well and garnish with a piece of pineapple if you wish!

CUCUMBER COOLADE

So refreshing ... and so good for you too!

1 Add all of the ingredients to the bowl of a blender or food processor and blend until smooth.
2 Serve in Kilner® Handled Jars over extra ice cubes and enjoy!

* How to deseed a cucumber: Use a sharp knife to cut the cucumber in half lengthways. Using a teaspoon, scoop out the seeds, avoiding the flesh by simply running the teaspoon gently down the centre of the cucumber.

Serves 2
1 cucumber, deseeded*
  and sliced
2 tbsp xylitol or stevia
Juice of 1 lime
Pinch of salt
Handful of ice cubes, plus extra
  to serve
400ml water

BURSTING BERRY SMOOTHIE

Made in minutes, just blend and serve!

1 Peel and chop the banana, then add to a blender, smoothie maker or food processor. Add the ice, spinach and berries. Blend until smooth.
2 Add a little water, a tablespoon at a time to give your desired consistency. Blend for another 10 seconds to mix.
3 Divide between 2 glasses and serve.

Serves 2
½ small ripe banana
Handful of ice cubes
Handful of washed spinach
50g raspberries
50g blackberries
50g strawberries, hulled

INDEX